HARDSCRABBLE LODGE

True Maine bush flying stories

Jake Morrel

Hardscrabble Lodge

True Maine bush flying stories

ISBN: 978-1-63381-082-2

Cover designed by Amy Files

Designed and Produced by

Maine Authors Publishing

558 Main Street, Rockland, Maine 04841

www.maineauthorspublishing.com

Printed in the United States of America

Hardscrabble Lodge would not have been possible without the energy and talent of my wife, Beth. None of the adventures described on the following pages would have occurred without her tireless effort. Our lives were enriched by these experiences. Thanks so much, my dear!

CONTENTS

GLOSSARY

◇◇◇

Below are the meanings of some words and phrases as used in the stories. Some are terms peculiar to Maine.

Aeronca sedan A four-passenger airplane manufactured by Aeronca after WWII.

amphibious airplane An airplane with retractable wheels mounted in the floats that can touch down on land or water.

Baxter State Park A large state park in northern Maine, made possible by Governor Baxter, and designated as forever wild.

Beaver A seven-passenger bush plane manufactured by DeHavilland.

budworm An insect that invades the Maine fir forest about every forty years.

bug dope A foul-smelling liquid designed to repel bugs.

cape a deer To remove the entire hide in one piece for taxidermy.

CL-215 A large Canadian amphibious airplane designed to drop one thousand gallons of water at a time on forest fires.

Coleman lantern A light fueled by gasoline which combusts around a silk mantle producing a brilliant light.

come-along A tool with a ratchet lever used to apply large forces to lift or pull.

dead water A section of a river with little current.

deer yard A place where deer congregate in the wintertime.

devil bug A small red-and-white dry fly.

Downeast The more northern coast of Maine. Originally, this was a sailing term since the prevailing winds tended to push ships toward that area. They were said, "to sail down east."

dunnage Luggage or freight.

evening rise When fish begin to feed heavily just before dark.

felt pack A heavy rubber boot lined with thick felt.

fen The part of eastern England that was drained with steam pumps to make farmland.

field dress To remove the internal organs from an animal in the woods before transport.

float or pontoon The structure that floats an airplane.

Folsom's Air Service A floatplane and skiplane flying service in northern Maine founded by Dick Folsom after WWII.

gas refrigerator A refrigerator that utilizes the energy in a propane flame to chill food.

glacial pond Ponds carved out during the last ice age that often have original strains of brook trout.

gravity water Water which flows downhill in a pipe from a high-enough elevation to produce normal domestic water pressure.

high lift jack A heavy-duty jack designed to lift up to three feet high.

ice out When the wintertime ice first clears a pond or lake.

Indian bar A segregated bar in northern Canada catering to native people.

L-4 A small WWII observation plane.

lobster pound A large pen in the ocean built to store live lobsters.

magneto A device that fires spark plugs without the need for a battery. Magnetos are used in airplane engines.

Maine Forest Service The Maine bureau responsible for fighting forest fires.

Maine guide or registered Maine guide An individual licensed by the State to guide guests.

moose sled A long sled pulled behind a snowmobile, used to move freight.

no-see-um Very small insects with a burning bite.

nubble or black nubble A small raised elevation of spruce and fir. The coloration is actually dark green.

over-boost To pull more power from a supercharged airplane engine than permitted by the manufacturer.

paper company lease The only way to acquire a place to live or operate a business in the Maine woods.

partridge Maine term for ruffed grouse.

peavey A tool used to roll logs. It has a four-foot handle with a large metal hook and point at the bottom end.

pick pole A sixteen-foot log handle fitted with a metal end and used for pushing pulp logs on the water.

pulp truck A heavy truck designed to haul wood and fitted with a loading crane.

purlin A horizontal log supporting a roof.

radial engine An airplane engine with the cylinders arranged in a circle.

saddle A level narrow passageway between two higher elevations often containing deer trails.

Scott Paper company The principal landowner around Hardscrabble. This paper company did not sell any land. Everyone who had a cabin or business leased.

skidder A machine with seven-foot diameter tires designed to haul trees across rough ground.

spell each other Maine term meaning to give the other person a rest.

Sporting Camp, Camp, Lodge Businesses which host guests in the Maine woods. A camp with a small "c" is private.

Sportsman Show Large events hosted in bigger cities showcasing hunting and fishing businesses.

spud A tool resembling a large dull chisel, used to peel bark from logs.

straight ahead or straight out A Maine expression meaning busy.

Supercub A two seat STOL (short take off and landing) aircraft manufactured by the Piper Aircraft Company. Jake used a 1953 model equipped with floats or skis at Hardscrabble.

taildragger An airplane with the steering wheel in the rear.

Taylorcraft A manufacturer of small airplanes before and after WWII.

tracked vehicle A military surplus M42 Weasel which went in snow and steered like a bulldozer.

union suit One-piece long underwear, usually made of red wool.

wild brook trout Trout species that have never bred with hatchery fish.

Willys A four-wheel drive vehicle designed for WWII and usually called a jeep.

PROLOGUE

◇◇◇

Beth and Jake End Up in the Woods

What would prompt my wife Beth and me to move our young family deep into the woods? After all, I was flying floatplanes for Folsom's Air Service, my dream job. We lived in a comfortable home in Greenville and were a happy family. 1978 was a pivotal year.

It *was* true that Beth and I had always sought adventure and challenge. Neither of us was cut out for conventional, suburban life. But our experience in the air service, and exposure to other families making their homes in the remote Maine forest, was most influential. Many times I ferried guests to those camps, chatted with owners, and listened to customers rave about lodge life. Beth and I saw the advantage of self-employment, plus an ideal setting in which to raise our children. (Our hunches proved true. At mealtimes, Thea and Zeke listened to adult conversation, such as: a photographer describing the challenge of filming a beaver felling a tree; a judge relating mistakes of judgment; a successful industrialist confiding how he hated his life; and once someone said, "You two kids have no clue how lucky you are." Our children also became mini-entrepreneurs, selling worms and waiting on tables; learning to cherish tips.)

As a pilot, I loved the concept that the floatplane was essential for operation of the camps. We would live like settlers in my favorite Alaskan stories!

It took, however, a couple decades to stumble upon that way of life, and perhaps the course had its genesis in my birthplace, a rural section of Pennsylvania. The landscape was beautiful: small farms and wooded lots. My childhood was nature-oriented, and early on, my parents let me roam the fields and forests. Our neighbors were a mix of folks who made a living with their hands and professionals who commuted some distance to the city. My father had grown up in the Depression, worked his way through college, and graduated with a chemical engineering degree. He worked for DuPont; my mother was a homemaker. We were a typical 1950s boom family.

Nothing was more important to my parents than academic achievement, with perfection the only acceptable outcome. My brother enjoyed intellectual pursuits. I, on the other hand, worked hard enough to get decent grades but tended to be a bit wild. By the time high school rolled around, the rebel crowd had attracted my attention. Sneaking out at night to sip quarts of beer was more fun than Emily Dickinson. My girlfriend, the future valedictorian, was the daughter of the longtime school secretary. The two of us would skip school, and her mother forged our notes. My dad was not pleased when we were caught!

One day he announced that I was bound for a Quaker school in Poughkeepsie, New York. We fought and argued at length about the decision. My young heart was broken. No more fun, no more friends! Of course my parents prevailed, even though I threatened to run away from the school.

Surprisingly, after a few days at Oakwood, I changed my mind. The student body was quite diverse compared to rural Pennsylvania; only a few students were Quakers; many were Jewish, many were black. Best of all, the school was coed, so the social scene was active. My first year went well: a steady girlfriend, lots of sports, and decent grades.

The first day of my second year included a major foreshadowing event. New students were assigned to sit with volunteer hosts at lunch, in order to help them adapt. Across my table sat a striking girl. She did not have classic, pretty-girl features, but her face was magnetic, along the lines of Sophia Loren.

Beth and I became good friends, but never dated. Probably wise, as I was reverting to my bad habits and was lucky to survive those last two years. Somehow, Tufts let me sneak through its doors into the engineering program.

To make a long story short, I had not learned my lesson. After two years with good grades but poor behavior—expulsion. My father was furious. After he cooled, he helped me gain admission to the University of Maryland's engineering school.

Academic Dean Elkins, realizing that a challenge was in order, looked into my eyes and stated, "Your acceptance is conditional. You must stay on the Dean's list, and at the first hint of trouble, you are out that door. Do you understand?"

"Yes, sir."

Coincidentally, Beth had enrolled at the Maryland Institute of Art located in Baltimore. At Oakwood, I had been, as is said—the big fish in a small pond. Now, I was one of 50,000 students, didn't know a soul, had no car, and was under a mandate to perform academically. The thought of a beautiful girl, whom I admired, living just thirty minutes away, was intoxicating. A phone call did the trick; we had a date! The first led to others, then romance, followed by our engagement. During the fall of my senior year we stood before the altar of the people's church (The National Cathedral), as husband and wife. With her firm guidance, I achieved the grades and remained in control.

After working at a co-op summer job with DuPont for three years, one fact became clear: engineering was the wrong choice. So Beth and I applied for teaching jobs at private schools: Beth in art, and I in math and physics. My introduction letter was blunt. Every mistake was described from high school through

Tufts. Miraculously, we were asked to come to Maine for an interview.

Hinckley School was a dream come true. Set on a 2500-acre rural campus with 200 students, the program stressed sports and outdoor activities. Busses of students were regularly driven all over Maine to ski, recreate on the coast, hike, and so on. We were hired. Through the school, Beth and I traveled through most of Maine. We were drawn to two areas of our new state: the bold Downeast Coast and the expansive wilderness of northern Maine. Both locations, beautiful and unspoiled, would factor into our future.

Tommy, a Hinckley maintenance worker, was an airplane nut. His father had been an early bush-pilot in Greenville. One day, Tommy arranged for his friend Herb to give me a ride in a 1946 Taylorcraft BC 12D—a small 65-horsepower, side-by-side taildragger. I was surprised when Herb started the engine by spinning the propeller by hand. No electrical system was installed! As we taxied prior to takeoff, normal conversation was difficult, the seat was a shaking canvas sling, and the smell of burning oil and fuel penetrated my nose. When the throttle was advanced, we were airborne in seconds and climbed rapidly. Unlike an airliner, the small craft was buffeted by constant air currents. The pilot idled the engine to demonstrate that we glided without power. No sense of choking fear grabbed me; the bird's-eye view was mesmerizing. Flying felt like my calling.

At the time, small, older airplanes cost less than two thousand dollars, about the same as a VW beetle. Eighty-octane aviation fuel was 35 cents a gallon; there was no charge to tie a plane next to the grass strip; and yearly maintenance was a couple hundred dollars. Flying was affordable!

Smitten after the flight, my search for a set of wings commenced, and success came soon: a 1946 Taylorcraft BC12D was for sale. Beth was lukewarm, but reluctantly agreed. The bank said yes, and we became a one-plane family.

Flying was practical on skis in the winter, followed by wheels come spring. Float flying was the dream of most local pilots because Maine had so many ponds and lakes accessible only by air. A seaplane opened a whole new world. However, pontoons were scarce. No small sets had been manufactured in years. Finally, two sets of damaged Edo 1320s (which fit our plane), were advertised. I jumped at the opportunity. Over two years, the non-functional floats morphed into one respectful set. The precise work was enjoyable.

Dick Folsom (the legendary bush-pilot from Greenville), signed off on the float rating. From that point on, the Taylorcraft flew constantly. Subsequently, commercial, instructor, and instrument licenses filled my billfold. Fortunately, I could satisfy flying time requirements to earn the ratings in my own plane. My flight instructor charged eight dollars an hour.

After five years, it was obvious that Hinckley School was on a downward course. Enrollment dropped, the charismatic headmaster had resigned, and money was tight. Beth and I decided to leave, but were appreciative of our first job experience. Our young children, Thea and Zeke, had been born at Hinckley. They played regularly with about twenty other faculty brats, and Beth and I had become good friends with the parents. A babysitter was always available! However, a new plan for our lives was in order.

Seeking an adventurous experience, Beth and I decided to move farther north to Greenville, the seaplane center of Maine. With a commercial license, a full-time pilot's job was possible. The back-up plan: part-time jobs in the recreational industry. Luckily, all fell into place. Eventually, Dick Folsom took a chance and gave me my dream job. The older, more experienced pilots were great mentors, to whom I'm sure I owe my life. Every day was a challenge, but also rewarding.

As I said initially, our years in the woods stand out. We were a young family working side by side, accepting the drudgery of hard work that led to the pleasure of success, meeting interesting people, and able to keep our heads above water. Years later, following the sale of our lodge, I used to sit at my desk in a machine shop, dreaming of Hardscrabble. I hope the tales that follow will explain why. Enjoy!

CHAPTER 1

◇◇◇

Instant Silence

Before we operated Hardscrabble, I spent eight years honing my flying skills. So first, a few chapters from the Folsom Air Service days...

Allow me to jump ahead for a moment and tell you that most fishermen arriving for a week of vacation at Hardscrabble were somewhat reserved in the beginning. They reacted as would a guest invited to a cocktail party who doesn't know everyone present. But after a couple of days, customers felt comfortable and mingled freely with the other guests, Beth, Carl, and me. Most peppered me with questions about remote life. And, sooner or later, almost all asked the same question, "Jake, has this plane ever quit on you?"

The answer was easy. "No!"

During hundreds of flying hours and thousands of takeoffs, the engine in the Hardscrabble Supercub had always performed flawlessly. Guests found that fact comforting.

If the question had been phrased differently—"Jake, has a plane engine *ever* quit on you?"—the answer would have been different. Twice, I experienced instant silence, which is twice as often as almost all other pilots. One failure occurred when I was a green student; the second was several thousand flight hours later in Greenville.

Small aircraft engine failures are rare. The plane and engine are designed with many redundant features. For instance, most bush planes have a gravity fuel system composed of two separate tanks. So, there is no fuel pump to fail. Each tank is fitted with a bottom drain so any accumulated water or debris can be drained. Usually, the gasoline passes through three different filters before it enters the cylinders. Every cylinder has two spark plugs, and the engine is equipped with two magnetos to generate powerful sparks. The magnetos will fire even if the battery is completely dead, since a rotating magnet generates the energy. As a result, reliability is built in.

Most airplane crashes occur because the pilot either cuts corners or makes bad decisions. Continuing a flight into deteriorating weather, exhaustion of fuel, and tired airmen are leading causes. Pilots worry about the engine when they should worry about themselves. If the fuel is not drained, or if extra gas is not added, the redundancies are defeated. In rare instances, however, good design fails.

I learned to fly in a 1941 Taylorcraft BC-65 on skis. Dick Flewelling, my instructor, was a middle-aged man with extensive experience. He was patient and gifted with the ability to explain complicated tasks clearly. Dick performed excellent demonstrations of the right and wrong way to execute each phase of flight. He also demanded that his students pay strict attention to procedure and practice maneuvers until they became second nature.

The combination of the skiplane and the solidly frozen Kennebec River created a great playground. I could take off, climb to 500 feet, then glide in for a landing repeatedly, along the eight-mile stretch next to the Poverty Flats airfield. Landing with different views each time taught judgment that simply orbiting an airport could not. Also, a student could touch down many more times per hour.

The long, wide river was the ideal place to practice engine failure for real. Dick sometimes shut off the fuel flow and killed the engine. After he demonstrated the procedure, I realized that a powerless Taylorcraft flew and landed nearly normally, though it descended more rapidly than when the motor was idling. We made repeated landings without power.

One morning, we took off from the airport to practice. About 300 feet into the air, without Dick's help, the motor failed completely.

I turned toward Dick, who sat with both arms across his chest. "She is yours!" I said.

He did not move a muscle. "You are the pilot of this plane," he replied.

No time to think! We were over a snow-covered pasture and sinking rapidly. Training kicked in automatically. I made a decent landing and quickly glided to a stop.

Dick, arms still unmoved, said, "Good job!"

When I climbed out of the Taylorcraft, my legs were weak. But great instruction paid off!

That engine failure was caused by ice crystals clogging a fuel filter. If an airplane tank sits partially filled outdoors, hoar frost forms on the upper interior surface of the tank. We had taxied a long way on rough snow before takeoff. The sloshing fuel had washed crystals into the fluid. After draining the gas several times, I took off and returned the plane to its tie-down.

Years later, when I flew out of Greenville, instant silence returned, this time in a floatplane. We had one plane that sometimes started with protest. With three passengers aboard, I climbed into the pilot's seat while the dock attendant pointed the Cessna toward open water. When the engine was cranked, it backfired once before starting and idling smoothly. We taxied in circles around the cove while the engine warmed on the cold morning. After a few minutes, we took off heading north up the lake.

After about a mile, without warning, no engine!

"Grab the seat in front of you with both hands," I instructed the passengers, trying to not sound panicked. "We'll make a normal touchdown straight ahead."

Landing was uneventful due to the prayers of the passengers.

"Now grab life preservers; I'll be right back."

I hopped out on the pontoon. *Crap, a crackling noise coming from the engine cowling. It's gotta be a fire.* I unsnapped the required fire extinguisher and aimed the discharge through the gap behind the exhaust pipe toward the small fireball. That worked! If the blaze had persisted, our only choice would have been a cold swim.

We were now floating around on a frigid day with a lake temperature not far above freezing. Fortunately, good Samaritans appeared quickly.

"Folks, as you can see, several boats are speeding toward us. You'll be on dry land in no time."

Within minutes, a boat docked next to the floats. A kind man hauled the passengers back to Greenville.

That engine-out was caused by a component failure. The backfire had loosened a tube that connects the left and right intake manifolds. The tube was secured with a rubber connector and tightened by expanding clamps. After reinstalling the tube, the motor ran smoothly.

Fortunately, my two failures occurred in ideal locations. However, Dick's thorough training prepared me to react—in the ideal manner—and probably gave me the confidence to even contemplate owning a lodge where flying every day would be the norm.

CHAPTER 2

◇◇◇

Mercy Flights

Today, if anybody is seriously injured in the more remote parts of northern Maine, the Life Flight helicopter is dispatched from Bangor. Aboard is a trained medical crew, and the aircraft is equipped just like an ambulance. Survival rates have soared since its inauguration. Forty years ago, however, Folsom's Air Service was the only option to rescue the injured. Three unusual trips come to mind from that era.

On an extremely windy day, a radio call came through from the Allagash Waterway Ranger.

"Got a teenager with a compound fracture of the lower leg who needs immediate care. Can you respond and save him a three-hour truck ride? Kid's name is Brad."

"I know the wind's so high all scheduled flights have been postponed, but anyone up for going?" Dick asked.

"I'll go," I volunteered.

As a precaution, we loaded the Cessna 185 with extra gas, knowing that the flight into the wind would add to the total flight time.

Two-foot swells rolled down Moosehead Lake next to the dock. We selected the first plane in line to make a straight-out departure possible. As I sat in the cockpit warming the engine, a fellow pilot stood by ready to release the ropes. Several minutes later the Cessna was set free. After a porpoising taxi (pontoons rising with the crests and slamming into the troughs), the

300-horsepower Continental engine roared to life. A couple of bumps on top of waves and the 185 was airborne, but going nowhere! The ground seemed to barely move underneath; the ride was rough. My seat belt was pulled as tightly as possible. For nearly an hour the plane flew north. Finally, Churchill Lake lay just ahead. The ranger had transported the boy to a shoreline in the lee of the blow.

My heart sank when I saw the boy. He was in severe pain, sweating profusely, and in and out of it. Blood soaked through his pant leg. His complexion indicated a young teen, but the poor kid acted like a tough adult. We loaded him into the copilot's seat under a blanket. I took the ranger aside.

"I don't know how this is going to be for the kid; the air is violent."

"I know, Jake, we have a lousy choice here. But the road is rough as hell this time of year. It would take at least two and one-half hours in the pickup. At least you'll get there in 30 minutes."

I climbed into the cockpit, taxied out, and headed south.

"Brad, buddy, I know you're hurting, but listen up. We are covering ground with the wind at 150 miles an hour. I'll be able to see Moosehead in ten minutes. I've got this plane balls to the wall. Just hold on, we're going to get you to a hospital with pain killers."

Brad never replied.

Fortunately, we were roaring over the ground with the wind on our tail, but every time the plane bucked, the teenager moaned.

An ambulance waited at the dock. Dick had assembled a crew to ease the Cessna into the float. By running the motor at a certain RPM, and maneuvering the controls, it was possible to "sail" sideways toward the crew. They grabbed the wing and secured the aircraft. Within minutes the patient was on a stretcher under a doctor's care. What a relief!

The second incident occurred early in the spring. Two men were hypothermic on Chamberlain Lake. Telford, a senior pilot, and

I, headed that way. We reasoned that two might be required to load the patients. The sight that greeted us on the beach was surreal. Two overweight, middle-aged men in shorts and tee shirts were soaking wet, sitting in shallow water, splashing each other. Two younger, much smaller, athletic-looking women were attempting to move them to shore, but their friends fought the effort.

We approached the two.

"Fellas, you need to get into the plane."

They attempted to rise but couldn't. They babbled incoherently. One lay down!

Telford walked next to me and said in a low voice, "We have to wrestle them one at a time into the plane."

We grabbed the first while the women attempted to move the second. Essentially, we man-handled him into the plane. Once inside, he lay back on the seat. All four of us loaded the partner. The girls wrapped their dates in our blankets.

One of the women handed Telford two wet wallets.

Telford cruised to Greenville at a high-power setting. Again, the ambulance was waiting. The final outcome in this case is unknown. The patients were transferred to the regional hospital in Bangor, fighting for survival. We never heard if either lived.

The last event falls into the category of unbelievable. A message arrived that a group of campers needed an emergency shipment of supplies. A long list was attached, detailing dozens of bottles of bug dope and long-sleeved women's shirts, in a range of sizes. I nearly bought out Sanders Store, all on credit. Maine is a buggy place during May and June. Black flies and mosquitoes can literally surround a person in a swarm.

Unfortunately, a South Carolina camp for teenage girls had planned a one-week canoe trip in Maine—without that salient knowledge! The group was paddling on Ciss Stream and was miserable. The organizers, knowing little about the state, had specified short-sleeved shirts and had not packed insect repellent!

When I landed on the stream the girls treated me like a conquering hero. They were outfitted in matching uniforms: khaki shorts and white, short-sleeved T-shirts with a snappy logo. Every arm and leg was covered with bites. I distributed the care package and hoped for the best.

As a footnote, Dick Folsom had a big heart. Numerous times we were summoned because someone thought someone else was experiencing a heart attack. Almost always, the problem was indigestion. Of course, we immediately responded. His goodness was not always appreciated. Too many of those passengers refused to pay our bill, claiming that someone else had ordered the flight.

CHAPTER 3

◇◇◇

Jake, Breaking and Entering—Twice!

Between Greenville (on the south end of Moosehead Lake), and the top of northern Maine, several ridge lines cross the state from west to east. When warmer, humid air arrives in the summer, thunderstorms spawn along these elevations and move in lines north to south. Floatplane pilots try to plan trips early in the day in order to avoid the afternoon buildups. On long trips, often the only alternative is to land in a sheltered spot and wait out the storms.

One particularly nasty, hot day, we got a radio call reporting an unspecified emergency at Round Pond on the Allagash Wilderness Waterway. Round Pond is one of several permitted landing sites on the protected river. I fueled and took off for the one-and-a-half-hour round trip.

Thunderstorms boomed everywhere. Often the air between cells was calm, but close to cloudbursts, intense downdrafts spilled out at ground level in all directions. Zigzagging east and west, I finally approached Round Pond.

Waiting at the campsite were an older doctor and a young nurse. They were both outfitted straight from the LL Bean catalog; however after several days on the river the new clothes were dirty and smelled of sweat, wood smoke, and bug dope. She explained that they had planned a longer canoe trip, but had capsized and lost most of their provisions. The man was soaked to the skin and looked very cold. Early in the summer, the water temperature is still frigid even though the air temperature has soared.

The young woman, Elizabeth, took me aside and whispered, "We have to get Walt to Greenville. He is hypothermic."

I quickly loaded them and their gear into the Cessna.

"There's a blanket stowed in the baggage compartment I can get for him," I said.

Walt made light of the situation, although his speech seemed somewhat sloppy.

I headed south, and within ten minutes a wall of black clouds and lightning loomed ahead.

"It'd be foolish to attempt a detour left or right. A sheltered cove for refuge is our only choice," I told them.

"Really? There's no way around this? We really need to get to a health facility as soon as possible," she said.

"Elizabeth, I understand the emergency. However, this plane won't survive a flight into that wall of violent turbulence. The storm will pass quickly. Let's concentrate on warming Walt. We can break into that camp to the right."

We landed and secured the floatplane with long ropes. Walt could barely climb out of the aircraft. Rain poured down. I swung Walt's arm over my shoulder and Elizabeth did likewise. He was wrapped in an increasingly wet blanket. We made for the camp.

No one was around, and the door was secured with a heavy-duty padlock.

"What are we going to do?" asked Elizabeth. "What are we going to do?"

"Let me look around, and I'll try to force our way in. We have no choice," I said, as we lowered a shivering Walt to the ground.

I found a discarded piece of steel under the building and pried off the lock, breaking the door trim in the process. Once inside, Elizabeth and I found dry wood and kindling and built a blazing fire in the woodstove. Elizabeth located a stack of Hudson Bay wool blankets in the bedroom closet.

"Why don't you hug him, while I wrap you together in the blankets, like a cocoon," I said.

Before long, his shivering subsided, and the crisis had passed.

Within an hour, the skies cleared, leaving hundreds of little white puffs in the tops of the trees.

"I'll leave a note with phone numbers and names," I said. "Folsom's will pay to repair the door."

About a week later, Connie opened a nasty letter from the cabin owner.

"They're threatening to press charges!" she said.

She called and explained the situation, but to no avail. I flew a carpenter into the camp, and soon the door looked new. They never took court action, which in Maine would have been futile. In remote areas, the Good Samaritan Law, codified in Maine, limits personal liability in extreme emergency, and is interpreted liberally.

My next break-in had nothing to do with weather.

A 50-something year-old man with a runner's physique bounced into Folsom's office one day to inquire about a floatplane ride. His attire caught my attention. Most ride customers arrived in printed T shirts, shorts, and running shoes. This individual wore a dress shirt, tailored pants, and expensive loafers. His wife trailed behind.

"How much would it cost to fly to Katahdin, circle for 15 minutes, and return?"

"We charge by the plane-hour, Sir, so that would be about an hour trip at $150 an hour," Connie replied.

"Wow! These little planes aren't cheap, are they? But I'll tell you what. I'm going to bite the bullet and go anyway. Do you take credit cards?"

"We'll take cash, credit cards, gold, whatever you have. One time Dick traded a short flight for six lobsters," Connie quipped. "Sir, Jake here will be your pilot. You may have to tell him how to get there. No, just kidding. I think Jake was born in a plane."

We shook hands, and he introduced himself as Ralph.

"Ralph, your wife can ride along for free since we charge by the hour," I suggested.

"Jake, I don't think two of your local lumberjacks could drag my wife into that floatplane. She is uncomfortable in jets, and thinks small planes are downright dangerous."

"Understood," I replied.

"When I was in my 20s," he said, "I hiked all through Baxter State Park, and I've always wanted to view my trek from the air."

As we walked down toward the dock, I mentioned how lucky Maine people are to have such a treasure in their backyard. "One man, Governor Baxter, fought tooth and nail to create this wonder, and paid for much of it from his own pocket. My wife and I have climbed several of the peaks within the park. People come in every summer to take a flight to the mountain. Many were last there as kids, forty or fifty years ago."

We headed toward Katahdin. The air was clear, but somewhat bumpy. Ralph was excited as we circled the mountain several times. He remembered the names of several trails which I located for him. He was amazed to see how short the treks looked from above. Soon we were headed home.

Halfway back, he grew quite ill. I landed on Crawford Pond, helped him out of the plane, and he lay down on a nice beach, a few yards from an unoccupied cabin. After about 30 minutes his color returned.

"I think I'm ready to fly," Ralph said.

We walked back to the Cessna. I pushed the tail off the sand and hopped aboard. When I flipped the master switch on, silence—no gyro windup, no radio static, no lights!

"The battery is completely dead," I informed Ralph. "This problem has happened before, but the mechanic swore it was cured. Sorry, we'll just have to wait."

"What? Can't you radio for help?" Ralph asked.

"The radio works off the battery. Listen, Connie, the dispatcher, knows our destination. She'll send search planes and they'll see our plane. It's five o'clock and daylight lasts until eight."

"Well, I'll take your word for it. Seems like Connie is right on the ball!"

By six-thirty, I was convinced that a miscommunication had occurred.

"Ralph, we're probably going to spend the night in that cabin. It's getting toward dark, so we ought to get situated while we can see. No big deal, maybe we'll even find a bottle of the owner's favorite booze. Let's have at it."

When I turned around, Ralph had tears in his eyes. All he said over and over again was, "Betty will think I've been killed. I can't stand the thought that she will feel hurt."

Not knowing what to do, I said, "Ralph, Connie will be with your wife. Every one of the planes has an ELT that sounds an alarm in the event of a crash. No alarm has sounded so they know no plane has gone down."

After a minute or so, Ralph seemed to absorb that statement and relax.

I broke into the camp, found some stored canned goods, and cooked dinner. Ralph did eat!

Just before dark, a sound interrupted the rhythmic cacophony of twilight bird chatter.

"I hear an engine!" I said.

We rushed outside to see a Cessna 206 circling Crawford and landing.

Out jumped George Later, head pilot from the Greenville Maine Fish and Game office.

"Jake!" he called. "Dick Folsom guessed the problem was the battery, and I've got a spare for you. About half a dozen planes have been searching for a couple hours."

After leaving a note, we were off to Greenville. Sure enough, our destination had been confused, so there was a huge area to scan.

Ralph was subdued on the way back. I could tell he was embarrassed, but also relieved. When we arrived at Folsom's, he and Betty rushed toward each other and hugged for what seemed like a minute. Following the embrace they exchanged a long, passionate kiss. Both had tear-streaks on their cheeks. All of us were touched by the display. Connie even hugged me!

Akin to Ralph and Betty's devotion, Beth and I had quite the partnership—both of us up for the adventure of a lifetime—creating a home in the wilds of Maine!

CHAPTER 4

◇◇◇

First Look at our Future Home

When I worked as a commercial floatplane pilot in northern Maine, it seemed as though horrible weather spawned customers who impulsively decided to take a flight. During the early fall of 1979, the company radio crackled to life with a request to fly four men from a lodge on Lobster Lake to Spencer Lake, 45 miles west. Under gray skies I took off into heavy wind-whipped swells, and headed north from Greenville to the pickup point.

The breakers on the beach at Lobster meant that the only practical way to come to shore was by turning the plane into the wind, shutting down the engine, and drifting backwards to the sand. The cheerful men from New Jersey greeted me; two were enjoying large cigars. It was apparent that cocktail hour had started some time before.

We bounced off the tops of the surf for a spell, finally became airborne, and swung toward a westerly course. From the banter during the flight, the purpose of the trip emerged. The oldest of the four, who appeared to be the ringleader, recounted his conversation with their host at the lodge.

"Last night, Stan told me that old camps rarely come up for sale, and that we ought to jump on this chance. He was there 25 years ago, and remembers a great location at the head of a three-mile-long pristine lake. Stan says the cottages should be easy to restore. Even if the roofs of the cabins are gone, he said the log walls will be sound. So for maybe 5K per building, plus say 20K to buy the lease, we all get individual camps. That's peanuts, you guys. We'll have a private retreat. Our old ladies won't have a clue what happens there!"

Never before had anyone requested a flight to that exact spot, so I was curious to view something new. Flying several circles over the remains of the camp showed that the builder had selected a great setting. The cabins were situated at a narrows between two lakes where a mountain stream tumbled into Spencer Lake, and were protected north, west, and east by 500-foot cliffs. On decent days the sun would pour in from the south.

Once on the ground and wandering through the remains, the sportsmen quickly lost all enthusiasm.

"Sound walls, bullshit! Half of these logs are toast, and forget the floors and roofs. Goddamn you, Stan! Wait 'til I nail his ass!" roared the spokesman. After less than ten minutes, they wanted to head back to the comfort of the large fieldstone fireplace in the lodge.

"Yeah, sure; this place is too far gone," I said, dishonestly seconding their opinion. We launched into the turbulent air for the return flight.

That evening, as usual, I told my wife Beth about the various flights that day, but did not dwell on the camp. The truth was that I had decided, while circling above the narrows, that Beth and I should buy the lease to the premises. So was planted the seed that led to our careers as sporting-camp owners and operators. Before continuing the story, let me give an explanation of the Maine term "sporting camp" and a brief discussion of their history in the state.

Before 1900, "rusticators" looked for remote locations to experience the "wilderness." Mostly wealthy men, their object was to view nature in a wild state but to live in comfort. Throughout northern

Maine, entrepreneurs, sensing an opportunity, restored and expanded logging camps or built new complexes. The guests became known as "sports" and the camps as "sporting camps." Most camps were sizable, and resembled small wilderness villages. In an era of cheap labor, many employees manned the operations. Guides, teamsters, cabin girls, and handymen were necessary. Staff tended large gardens, looked after teams of horses and milking cows, transported tons of supplies, cut ice in the winter, ran large laundries, pumped water, and tended to the guests' special requests.

Spencer Lake Camp had been a thriving business. The small village consisted of 16 guest cabins, dining facilities, barns, a warden's camp, plus a huge log building with a hardwood dance floor that was a personal cabin belonging to J. P. Morgan, the New York financier. The town was known as Gerard, Maine, and had its own post office.

So how did the guests and freight reach Gerard, 20 miles through the woods from the nearest road? The expansion of the railroad made the whole thing possible. Rail lines ran through Jackman, Maine, 30 miles away. From Jackman, guests took a private launch across Attean Lake, then a smaller boat up Moose River to Spencer Rips. There the luggage was put on a push, narrow-gauge railroad cart and arrived at the buckboard loading point, seven miles from the camp. A single-horse wagon was used to complete the trek. The entire journey took the better part of a day.

After a long debate, Beth and I decided to take a huge risk and pursue my dream. The abandoned buildings presented a great opportunity because we could substitute hard work for money we did not have and could not borrow. No bank at the time would lend all of the money necessary to fix up a derelict set of buildings in order to run a business that did not exist. By ourselves we had neither enough money nor enough manpower to pull it off. A partner was essential.

During the winters, I bartended at the local ski area to make ends meet. Carl Otley, a retired brick mason from Philadelphia, worked with me. Carl, ten years my senior, had a commanding presence. A blond Dane, he stood six foot four. His shoulders had broadened from years of lifting brick and block, and his large hands were those of a working man. Over one too many beers, we formed a partnership to attempt the purchase and immediately begin construction. Beth, myself, Carl, and his wife Marcy would have equal shares. The lease was listed at 55K. We decided our top offer would be 25K, and made an initial bid of 22K. To our shock, they accepted the initial bid. Like it or not, there was no turning back!

In order to open before June of the following year, we drew up a chronological list of the tasks ahead. We had to: locate and buy a small, powerful plane with both floats and skis; transport building supplies over the rough, four-wheel-drive road that wound 18 miles from the State road into the site; cut and split firewood for the coming winter; gather enough rocks to erect a stone fireplace in the main lodge; rebuild as much as possible before snow flew (in order to have weather-tight buildings so we could work on the interiors over the winter); buy boats, canoes, woodstoves, kitchen supplies, bedding, etc., required for operation. Then most importantly, we had to hit the road—for part of the winter—to attend sporting shows in New York, Philadelphia, Harrisburg, and Boston, in an effort to attract enough fishermen and hunters to make the venture a success.

As the four of us stared at the incomplete list, a sinking feeling was experienced by all. Had we doomed ourselves by setting totally unrealistic goals and time schedules? Would we run out of money? Would enough customers materialize? Being young with limited business experience, we did not have enough common sense to abandon the project. Instead, everyone plunged forward, working long days and tackling tasks as weather and seasons permitted.

Commercial bush flying had given me the opportunity to pilot a wide variety of float and ski planes. Our plane would be used for transportation to and from the lodge, and to haul our future guests to and from small remote ponds that hosted sustainable populations of wild brook trout. To fulfill the second function, a powerful engine coupled with a high-lift, slow-stall-speed wing were necessary. In our price range, an older Piper Supercub was the logical choice. By chance, one was for sale, sitting on floats in our hometown of Greenville, Maine. We bought the plane and separately purchased a set of AirGlas 2000 skis for winter operation. Write checkmark number one!

Long lists were assembled of the required supplies of lumber, masonry, plumbing, propane gas fittings, roofing, tools, and other hardware. Delivery of the materials presented a large hurdle. The volume of our order would require several trips with large trucks over a nearly impassable road.

"I have a suggestion," said John Morrell, the owner of our local building supply center. "How 'bout I approach local log haulers. They drive on rough woods roads to the north of town all the time. The trucks are probably going to get beat up, so I'll ask operators with old rigs. Can you pay enough to make it worth their while?"

We said we could, and two jobbers agreed to tackle the task, provided that we hired enough men to unload the full trucks quickly. Since logging trucks routinely carry payloads of 30 tons, six able men were contracted. Carl and I drove out in the jeep to meet the incoming load. We waited at the point where the road turned narrow and rough.

The first driver stopped when he saw us.

"What's going on? Why is he stopping?" I said to Carl.

"I don't know. Look; he's getting out."

The burley logger, disgust starkly written across his face, walked toward us.

"There's no way in hell, I'm going any further. Unload my truck," he said.

"What?" was all I could come up with.

"Here. Now. Unload my truck."

"Bud, we are not touching one stick of that load! You were hired to deliver the lumber to Spencer Lake. We have absolutely no way to move all this shit the last eight miles. It's either Spencer Lake or turn around and head her back out!"

"You two have totally screwed me! I can't turn around, no room."

After heated discussion, not appropriate for young audiences, he continued the rest of the way.

The second driver was locally known as a wild man and brawler. He drove a truck that appeared to belong in a salvage yard. Arriving at the camp, beer in hand, he laughed at our description of the road as rough, claiming he drove on worse every day. While the crew unloaded a heavy cargo of concrete blocks, he and his friend sipped additional beers. Empty and light, the old truck quickly accelerated as it began the long climb out of the valley. Since the driver had torn off a mirror on the way in when he was relatively sober, I was concerned about the return journey. A short hop in the plane confirmed my fears. The rig was abandoned, spanning a washout, and the driver and passenger were walking back. We headed toward the two in an old Willys jeep.

Just ahead, both men sat on a rock, taking a rest while opening another beer.

"Jake Morrel, I ought to pound your ugly face in! You told John Morrell that this road was just like our roads up north. Bull shit! This is nothing but a goat path."

"Wilbur, not half an hour ago, you said the road was a piece of cake. What's changed all of a sudden?"

"Hey, don't wise-ass me or you WILL swallow your teeth."

Since the man loved to fight, I wanted to avoid trouble. No need getting beat up and then being unable to swing a hammer!

"Look, I'll fly both of you to Greenville," I said. "We can work things out with the truck later."

I flew them out and never heard another word. (Later, I learned that his mechanic repaired the truck on the spot and drove it out to the highway.) Write checkmark number two.

Fortunately, the slopes rising above the cabins were initially of gentle grade and covered with middle-aged hardwood—mostly maple, beech, and ash. Using an old Farmall tractor and four-foot log trailer, it was an easy task to cut trails and bring the needed firewood down to the camp yard. Since by winter the cabins would have woodstoves installed, the four-foot pieces had to be cut in thirds with chainsaws and the pieces split with mauls. Processing wood by hand is hard work, but mostly it's boring. Ten cords of finished firewood is made up of hundreds of pieces that have to be cut, split, and stacked. Everyone was glad when that chore was finished. Write checkmark number three.

Most hunting and fishing lodges feature oversized stone fireplaces with comfortable couches sitting within the warm zone. During the early fishing season after ice out, and throughout hunting in the fall, the Maine weather is often cold and damp. Drinks in front of the fire after a cold day in the field are certainly something to anticipate. The remains of the old lodge had no fireplace. Before early winter we needed to pour a foundation and gather rocks to surround the core of concrete blocks we'd had delivered.

Maine lakes normally recede in the fall, exposing rocky shorelines. We decided to cruise the perimeter of Spencer, selecting attractive stones, utilizing a small open boat. The prized specimens, which appear occasionally, have a square edge for a corner or an unusual texture or coloration. The grand prize is a keystone which will become the center stone of the fireplace arch. Gathering by boat went surprisingly rapidly since we toured by thousands and thousands of choices. After many trips, the rock pile was more than ample. At the same time, we gathered polished four-foot pulp logs, left high on shore after wood-drives years before. Even though wood had not been moved to the mills by water for years, the leftovers were totally sound. Write checkmark number four.

Closely scrutinizing the remains of the buildings, it was apparent that by repairing the best structures, using logs from the worst in addition to lumber that had been delivered, seven cabins could be salvaged. Abandoned log buildings rot from the earth up. Even if the roofs have collapsed, the upper logs are often sound. We ended up with a nice supply of repair logs, with a patina matching that of the best cabins. Unfortunately, none of them were long enough to become roof purlins (the long horizontal supporting logs). In order to make those, we had to cut straight spruce of the right size and peel the bark with spuds (a tool resembling a wide chisel but with a dull blade and longer handle to gain leverage). The purlins were then rolled up onto the roof on other sloping logs with peavies (a tool with a four-foot handle above a metal point and outfitted with a large hook next to the point). We nailed roof boards into place, installed roll roofing and created weather-tight buildings. Lastly, porches were added and some new windows fitted. Write checkmark number five.

"Uncle Henry's" is a Maine weekly publication of used items, running a couple hundred pages. By buying the paper as soon as it was distributed and carefully scanning the pages, over time we located the majority of supplies necessary for operation. An exception were the five boats and motors. For obvious reasons those had to be reliable. We decided to buy brand new ones.

The boats' journey into Spencer Lake was unusual. By the time Grumman processed the order, deep snow covered the ground. I decided to haul all five boats (for 18 miles), behind my double-track snowmobile. The distributor left them on the State road on top of a snow bank. With the boats tied together like railroad cars and the snow machine in the lead, the trip commenced. All went well until we arrived at Bear Hill, about halfway in. Bear

Hill is a continuous grade of five miles. Not too long after cresting the hill, the boats started making a noise. Looking back, I saw they were zig-zagging and sliding forward faster than the snowmobile was rolling. The only solution was acceleration. By the time the train reached the bottom of the hill, the throttle was full bore, but all was well. After five hours, the lake was in view. Write check-mark number six.

Before traveling south to lure customers, we prepared a draft color brochure. One important detail was undecided: what to name our new home? Beth suggested Hardscrabble, the mountain that sheltered the cabins. That stuck! We left with 5,000 copies of our literature.

Sportsmen shows, like trade shows for truckers or farmers, have a faithful following of the segment of the population sharing that interest. Fortunately, by attending shows, lodge owners can pitch their business to a captive audience. Some shows are huge. Harrisburg, Pennsylvania draws 500,000 enthusiasts over a ten-day period. Our challenge was to rent exhibit space on short notice in a visible location at each venue. Because I knew so many lodge owners who already had space (as a result of the float plane service), we succeeded in convincing the managers to give us a break.

The next challenge was to construct a rugged booth, unique enough to separate us from the huge crowds, plus attract attention—some shows have hundreds of exhibitors. Using extra salvaged logs, we constructed a three-sided log cabin with a shake roof. Using a chainsaw sawmill, we cut a pine slab 24 inches wide and three inches thick for a counter. For decorations, we adorned the walls with taxidermy and antique Maine-woods relics.

The finished product was successful. Frequently, after their first glimpse of the booth, people walked directly our way. Many groups of men expressed an interest in giving the lodge a shot. As the winter tour progressed, we took in more and more 50% deposits, and soon knew that the gamble would pay off. Mark check number seven.

We often had weeks in between shows to return to Maine. During those intervals, work progressed on the cabin interiors. Every time either the plane or the snowmobile went to camp, a full load of materials was ferried. We owned a ten-foot dogsled with a cargo box, so the snow machine could move a lot of weight. Also, the ski plane had a removable rear seat; about six feet of baggage area was created when it was gone. Over the course of the winter, all those loads made a huge difference.

The last show was in mid-March. Enough fishermen had laid down deposits to fill the lodge during the best part of the early fishing season, but the main building was far from finished. We worked ceaselessly, assisted by several good friends who stayed a week at a time. Different crews attacked the unfinished areas—the kitchen, the interior rock surface of the fireplace, the bar, and the front doors and screens. By the deadline of May 10th, the new facility looked pretty damn good!

CHAPTER 5

◇◇◇

Plane Liftoff—Minus the Pilot!

Flying in the most remote parts of northern Maine presented challenges and surprises. First, the pilot was on his own; no help was available by radio. The weather changed quickly, the snow surface switched from powder to frozen to flooded, and it was often very cold and windy. Plane engines did not start in cold weather unless preheated with a propane burner. Some of the situations we encountered during the first few seasons illustrate the danger.

Since the water level of Spencer Lake receded in the fall, the plane was tied down on the dry, sizable width of snow-covered, sandy lake bottom. The first winter, we had not constructed permanent buried anchors, so the Supercub sat in front of our cabin tied on each side to a cluster of three 150-pound propane gas cylinders.

Carl and I went to sleep at dark one night, after a long, exhausting day of reconstruction on the future Hardscrabble. A gentle breeze created a soothing sound as the tall pines' branches swayed outside.

I woke suddenly when the window next to the bed rattled. Obviously, the wind was blowing harder from the south, a sure sign of approaching bad weather. Quickly, sound sleep returned. Sometime later, a loud creaking noise jolted both Carl and I upright. The building shuddered and shook so violently, I feared for the recently installed new metal roof.

"Jake, we are #$##%#! This gale will wreak havoc!" Carl shouted.

"I know! But I don't care about the stacks of loose plywood or even the windows we didn't finish installing—I'm worried about the plane!" I yelled back. "That's valuable!"

I looked outside. "Holy $##%!" The intense beam of the six-volt flashlight illuminated a sickening sight.

The Supercub was dancing. Up it flew—about a foot above the ground, hopping slowly along, and dragging the cylinders. It would pause, then rise up again. It had moved about 100 feet in the direction of several large pine trees outside the door. Carl and I quickly dressed and raced toward the wing tie-down ropes.

Screaming above the roar of the blow, I yelled, "Pull toward the ice every time it lifts off!"

Two ants could have done just as well. The wind had tremendous power. At that moment I was sure our most important possession was lost.

Soon, we heard a sickening noise. One wing had contacted a tree trunk, and was sliding up and down the bark. We retreated inside, downed a couple shots of bourbon and lay back down. Neither of us slept, our spines rigid with each sharp crack emitted by the structure, and the constant roar. *What was going to happen next?*

Without planning to, we took turns getting up to look outside. The Supercub did not change position. By morning the worst was over, but rain fell steadily.

Unbelievably, the only damage was to the wing: an indentation about one foot wide and six inches deep. An airplane wing is designed with inspection holes in the outer surface fitted with covers. After removing several of these, no structural damage was evident. I was confident the plane would fly normally.

When decent weather returned, I took off for Greenville to make temporary repairs. Initially, I flew just over the surface of the ice, in case the damaged wing compromised control. Luckily, it didn't. The old girl was tough!

The next year, when the skiplane was tied to new, underground anchors, a heavy rain persisted for a couple days. When the sky finally cleared, the snow covering the dry lake floor had melted, and 50 feet of open water separated it from thick ice. The newly exposed beach was long enough for a takeoff on wheels, given a north wind, but the plane wore its winter skis. The only way to fly away was to take a snowmobile to the State road, find a ride to Greenville, pick up the airplane wheels, ride back in, remove the skis from the Supercub, and install the wheels. When the wind blew from the right direction, I took off and returned to Greenville.

After a few days of normal winter weather and a snowstorm, the 50 feet of open water iced over and new snow covered the lake bottom. The skis were reinstalled and travel resumed as before.

A third trial occurred before "ice out," a special event in Maine. Open water arrived in many ways. Sometimes ice cover miraculously vanished overnight. On other occasions, huge icebergs blew around for days battering the shorelines.

Jerry (my friend and helper) and I flew in on floats, even though most of the lake was frozen. Our location at a narrows meant that a long, thin segment melted very early, even though a foot or more of ice covered the majority of Spencer. We worked for several days, and then the wind switched to the south and was warm. The ice fragmented and moved as an enormous sheet, only halted when the leading edge collided with the bank. A long pile of sand was bulldozed by the mass. The Supercub, tied to shore in the long narrows, was safe.

That night it warmed some more, and the wind stiffened to a gale.

"Listen to that...we better take turns checking the plane ropes," I said.

"Sure," Jerry agreed. "I'll head out now."

Time for the last check before daybreak, and it was my turn. Tired, I rose from my bed, grabbed the flashlight, and headed outside.

After walking the 1,000 feet to the narrows, I pointed the flashlight beam toward the plane.

"Oh, my God!"

Large chunks of ice, each piece weighing tons, had broken free and moved down the narrows. I ran in the dark to alert Jerry, twice tripping on the rock-strewn beach.

Even before reaching camp, I yelled out, "Jerry! Jerry! Jerry!"

The door flew open before I arrived.

"The ice is piling against the plane. The upwind rope is stretched tight. We have to try and push the chunks away from the floats."

"Jesus, Jake, some of those weigh a ton."

"Jerry, this is our only shot. Grab a pick pole from under number-six camp. I'll get one off the wall in the lodge."

We ran for pick poles, left over from log drives in the past. The tool was 16 feet long and fitted with a metal point on one end.

After grabbing the handles, we hustled toward the narrows. Time to test our combined strength. We started with the mini berg on the outside of the jam. We pushed with all we had.

"Jake, it's moving!"

Very, very slowly, the mass of ice budged. Soon it drifted clear of the plane. Immediately, we tackled the second piece. Again, moving like a slug, it headed away. The tension in the upwind rope eased. We were winded and had just begun!

Pushing upwind of the plane, one by one, each mammoth berg eased away from shore just far enough to clear the plane floats. Hours later, our arms burning and sore, we stopped. The threat had passed; the ice was out. I would do anything to save my plane...

CHAPTER 6

◇◇◇

A Typical Long Day at Hardscrabble

Before dwelling on unusual events that occurred at Hardscrabble, let me describe our daily routine. Keep in mind that Beth and I were doing two things simultaneously: looking after our children (Thea, age 9 and her brother Zeke, 7), and running a business catering to about a dozen guests at one time.

From the beginning, both children were excited to be part of the business. Thea, because she was slightly older, proved to be extremely capable. At 9 years old, after learning to drive the 1953 Willys jeep, she'd meet Folsom's Air Service planes at the dock and drive the sports' luggage to the cabins. Thea also kept a notebook of needed supplies, as Beth dictated; and was the waitress, amassing over $1,000 in tips during her first summer. I was especially proud of Thea's guiding ability. She knew how to use a compass in an emergency, having practiced with me many times. Weather permitting, we flew fishermen to Little Enchanted Pond, but on foggy mornings, Thea walked with the men 2½ miles (uphill) to its shore, and returned by herself. (Many city guests were afraid to go by themselves.) Usually, she was paid at least $20. On another occasion, Thea paddled a canoe for a fly fisherman for a good part of a day.

During the endless floatplane trips back and forth to Greenville, I showed her basic piloting skills. By the end of the first season, given good weather, Thea could take off unassisted, find Greenville 40 miles away, and make a decent landing. Both children kept up with their homework, provided by the Greenville School System.

Our daily chores were divided between long- and short-term tasks. Most of the work on long-term projects occurred in the middle of the day when the fishermen or hunters were gone. A large garden had to be planted, tended, and harvested. All of next season's firewood needed to be cut and split. Routine plane and boat maintenance was essential. Bulk plane-gas and propane cylinders were ferried over the four-wheel-drive road. Cabins had to be cleaned, and bedding and towels washed and dried; many needed finishing touches. In short, there was plenty to do.

Daily events began at 4:30am. Beth prepared breakfast for 12, to be eaten at 7 AM, while I readied the plane and boats. Using a 5-gallon can and a raised platform we had constructed, gasoline was poured into the Supercub wing tank. (Throughout the day, small amounts of fuel were added so as to keep the plane as light as possible.) The outboard tanks of the boats were topped off, and shear pins were checked. Fishing line was removed if found tangled around any prop. Then, the time came to help Beth.

First, I had to awaken the fireplace. Many mornings, even in June, the air was cool. Zeke usually remembered to leave kindling on the hearth the previous evening. So given a combination of old coals, kindling, and new wood, a blaze typically took off quickly. Time to replace the fireplace screen. Walking into the cozy log kitchen, I always enjoyed the smell of freshly brewed coffee. After pouring a cup, I warmed the large griddle on the antique Garland propane range. My job was to grill dozens of pieces of sausage or bacon. Beth was fussy about their appearance. So while sipping from my cup, pieces were constantly rotated or flipped to avoid dark spots.

Soon, Thea would arrive to set tables (later, she hauled plates). We always had early risers who claimed they could smell food and coffee. The relaxed atmosphere meant the men felt comfortable walking into the kitchen and grabbing a cup. Quickly we learned to cook excess bacon because nobody could resist snagging an extra slice. For breakfast and dinner, only one menu was offered each day, rotating through different selections during the week. Without staff, that was our only practical alternative. (After breakfast, Beth prepared bag lunches for the sportsmen headed away for the day.) At 7:30, Thea served the men as each arrived. Fortunately, they tended to appear in small groups. As a result, no one usually waited very long.

Some readers may be curious as to why my partner Carl's name has not been mentioned in connection with breakfast. Carl and I quickly learned we had to divide the responsibilities of the day. In the evening, the men enjoyed swapping stories and lies over drinks in front of the fireplace. Many were night owls and stayed up past midnight. Carl enjoyed the banter and was a first-class storyteller. Since I had to fly early each morning, late nights were out of the question. (Carl's wife, Marcy, by the way, manned the phone and answered mail from their house in Greenville.)

After the last of the coffee, everyone departed by boat or plane. Hardscrabble was known for remote brook-trout fishing. A cluster of excellent "fly-fishing only" ponds were located within five miles of the camp. Canoes rode comfortably tied to the float struts of a Supercub, and we had flown 18-foot canoes into each pond. So taking one man at a time, I made the four-to-eight round trips of the morning. Carl assisted those who had chosen to fish Spencer Lake by boat.

Almost as soon as we opened, changes in two-way radio technology, led by Motorola, allowed us to communicate directly with Folsom's Air Service. This event was a game-changer. Now, each morning after the men left, we radioed in to check for new reservations or cancellations, order groceries to be sent in with the next flight, or make an occasional phone call. Connie, a long time Folsom employee, handled the radio. Her nickname was "the voice of the north woods." Connie patched in a phone call by placing the phone receiver over one shoulder and the radio microphone over the other. She then repeated what was said on the radio to the person on the phone, and vice versa. Crude, but it worked great. Connie knew everyone's business!

With the "sports" engaged, the lodge was unnaturally quiet. Well, not always! You learn early on that for some, fishing or hunting is just an excuse to leave home. It was not uncommon for guests to read all week or for a whole cabin of men to stay in and play cards. One particular type of visitor deserves mention. Some men wanted to be adopted. Basically, they wished to follow in your tracks all day long and help. That situation made it difficult to efficiently perform midday, long-term jobs, because although they meant to help, their skills were lacking. Watching someone attempt to swing a splitting maul for the first time is a scary sight. Generally, however, the middle of the day yielded valuable time for chores.

For Beth, midday provided time to spend with Thea and Zeke. Given a sunny day, she also looked after the laundry. We had no electricity, so the wash was done by hand and dried on a long clothesline. By early afternoon, it was time to start preparing the evening meal. All meals were cooked from scratch, and included a rotation of baked turkey, baked ham, shepherd's pie, lasagna, roast chicken, and meatloaf. Biscuits or popovers, fresh vegetables, salads, and desserts complemented the main course. We always looked forward to the evening meal. Beth performed miracles in that old log kitchen. Many guests commented that the fare was equal or better than that of the best restaurants they frequented at home.

As daylight faded, thus began my trips to return the fishermen to the lodge. Most serious anglers wanted to stay as long as possible, because the evening rise of the fish usually occurred toward dark. Often, during the last landing of the day, I could still see the water because the surface reflected light, but the shore was nearly dark.

Since the last anglers arrived home late, dinner was late as well.. The lodge had a pleasant atmosphere, lit by an array of gas lights and warmed by the fire. While the sports waited for biscuits, beer flowed easily, and the fishing tales began. As the night progressed, details were added to the original stories, and soon "one-upmanship" was the name of the game. The men kept a small notebook on top of the bar to keep track of their beer consumption. Our guests were always generous at week's end, paying for many more beers than they had consumed.

(The Anheuser Busch folks, brewers of Michelob, got wind of the remote, unusual bar and sensed a public relations windfall. They sent staff to Maine, flown in on the plane carrying the kegs, and bellied up to the bar. A photographer documented the trip. Later, an entertaining article appeared in their industry news magazine.)

After the evening meal, Carl made everyone feel at home. Card games were popular, as was the game of Cribbage. The large table near the fireplace had a Cribbage board drilled into its surface. As everyone settled in, Beth and I begged our leave. Once inside our cabin, we struggled to remain awake until Thea and Zeke dozed off. Our typical day had enough activity in it to keep us naturally fit and pining for a good night's sleep!

CHAPTER 7

◇◇◇

Water, Smoked Fish, and a Root Cellar

When the first guests arrived at Hardscrabble, they found a rather crude water system. Each cabin had a shower with hot water, but the spray was no more than a gentle rain. Pressure was generated by a water tower about 15 feet high. Perched on top of the structure was a war-surplus aluminum airplane fuel-drop tank (used for missions where the target was beyond the normal range of the aircraft). A dug well was located about 30 feet from our large mountain stream, whose flow filtered through sand and into the tile. The water was cold and had a pleasant taste. Several times a day, we had to start a generator and pump for half an hour to fill the huge tank. If someone left a toilet running overnight, the tank would be empty come sunrise. This did not please the sports eager for a "begin-the-day" shower.

I was determined to create a new system providing adequate pressure and unlimited volume. The solution was gravity water. The cold stream which spilled into the lake next to the lodge made this practical. Before a short, flat run near the camps, it cascaded down the east ridge, falling rapidly. A pool at least 50 feet in elevation above the lodge was necessary.

I knew, from hunting excursions, where the ideal candidate lay. It was composed of solid rock polished over the eons to a velvety-smooth surface. In the past, Thea and Zeke had enjoyed sliding down the slippery inlet and crashing into the deep water.

Measured by man paces, the source was approximately 3,000 feet distant. Using an old railroad sight level, I determined that the elevation was sufficient.

Money was very tight in the beginning of our operation. Initial expenses had been huge, and cash flow started as a trickle. Regardless, we purchased over 3,000 feet of one-inch diameter flexible polyethylene pipe. Several trips were required over the four-wheel-drive road to transport the numerous large coils and boxes of fittings.

On hot days, when the pipe was most flexible, we slowly unwound each coil along a narrow footpath up the mountain. Since Carl and I could only work a few hours in the middle of the day, the project stretched on for a week. Finally, a heavy filter screen was attached at the top, completing the system. A test of the gravity water was not possible until the next day.

We had not connected the last 300-foot section to the remainder of the run, so the siphon leaving the rock dam could be primed. We sealed the downhill end of the last segment, filled the last section using a bucket and funnel, and submerged the filter into the pool. Immediately, water rushed through the pipe.

"It's been an hour," I said, "and no water's coming out on the lodge end. What the heck is going on?"

"Let's walk the line," said Carl.

As we walked, we periodically lifted up the line to gauge weight. Empty! Finally, somewhat beyond the last section, it was heavy. I walked downhill along two 300-foot lengths and separated a connection. Pressurized air hissed out, followed very shortly by a stream of water. Two coil distances at a time, we established a hearty flow throughout the remaining pipe. Beth was monitoring the bottom end. Soon we heard her yell, "Water!"

Over many seasons the system functioned flawlessly. We had ample pressure, unlimited volume, and cold, fresh water. We drip-irrigated the garden in order to always maintain a fresh supply. The only repair was after a bear bit the line. At the end of October each year, I drained the pipe.

Another goal was to construct a smoker for Hardscrabble. Anglers enjoyed the novelty of eating their own smoked fish. After completing the new water works, the dug well was surplus. I shoveled a deep trench from the stream bank to the well. Since the bank was high above the water it would always stay dry. Next, using a masonry chisel, I fashioned a six-inch hole in the four-foot diameter well tile near the bottom of the ditch. A small wood stove nestled into the stream bank was connected by a six-inch stove pipe to the tile. The tile was fitted with a false bottom just below the pipe, stainless steel oven racks, and a small vent in the top lid.

We built a small fire in the stove using apple wood, and the smoke traveled the length of the pipe, filled the tile and exited through the top vent. Importantly, the smoke was chilled by the sand and the tile. If fish are smoked at too hot a temperature, the fat changes to oil and the result tastes terrible. The smoker saw regular use.

Usually we smoked fish for less than a day. That period infused flavor but did not preserve the flesh. Since the fishermen wanted to sample their catch without delay, the objective was accomplished. Harry, one of our guests, was so impressed with the taste of his smoked salmon that he asked to take samples home. We smoked his catch for three days and wrapped each fish in aluminum foil.

He wrote me a humorous letter upon returning to New York City.

Dear Jake and Beth,

Let me begin by saying that you two really surprised me. Last winter, when I read your brochure, the verbiage seemed a bit over the top. I found it hard to believe that for such a reasonable price I was going to be flown around each day, eat great food, plus enjoy hot showers and a comfortable bed. Call me dead wrong! You two offered much more than advertised. Please accept my reservation for the same week next year. Enclosed is a two-hundred-dollar deposit.

My wife is slightly cross with me! Don't get me wrong, she adored the smoked salmon. What irritated her was my smoked suitcase. Jake, she washed all of my clothes three times, and they still smell like smoked fish. Yesterday, she gave up and took me shopping. In a way, that is a good thing. Now she can't complain that my wardrobe is twenty years out of date.

My best to Thea and Zeke. Thanks for all the pleasant memories.

Harry

We learned from that experience!

Digging a root cellar by hand was another ambitious project! Nevertheless, the structure was vital, due to our remote location. I began to dig. In the early spring, a root cellar is cool enough to serve as a walk-in cooler. Also, on unusually cold nights in the very early spring, the inside temperature stays well above freezing. Most important, in winter the cellar is potentially a survival space. During the most frigid weather, an injured person, unable to maintain a fire, could crawl into the ground and avoid frostbite.

The logical location for the pit was next to the smoker, where the stream bank was the highest. Digging deeply into it, a three-sided excavation would require the least work. After many days, the pit was seven feet deep, eight feet wide, and twelve feet long. The substrate revealed ancient history. Toward the top were a couple of ash layers, while further down, several layers of pebbles emerged: fires and floods. We fashioned walls out of heavy, rot-resistant cedar logs, and then a ceiling in a similar manner. Last, a door was added facing the stream bank. The large piles of dirt surrounding the pit were heaped over the top using my antique bulldozer.

After constructing shelves along three walls, we had a useful, snug structure. It was always in use. Staples which couldn't be frozen were stored inside during cold weather. Large boxes of fresh vegetables lined the racks.

Fortunately, I never had to crawl inside and wait for help.

CHAPTER 8

◇◇◇

A Floatplane Can Transport *Anything*

Thirty or forty years ago, many lakes and ponds in northern Maine lay a long ways from a passable road. Numerous private camps and commercial lodges were located on those bodies of water. Often the residents of those remote areas would undertake projects requiring large volumes of material or freight to be ferried from Greenville to the site. This was when floatplanes saw use as trucks.

Four different types of planes were employed. A DeHavilland Beaver was the biggest, and could haul nearly a ton. That airplane was designed from scratch as a bush workhorse. Cessna 206s, 185s, and 180s, smaller but very capable, made up the rest of the fleet. Although the interior cargo space was adequate for much of the freight, often, bigger items had to be tied to the exterior. Each type of external freight had to be secured in a particular manner. What I'm about to describe was customary forty years ago. Today, the FAA has made it almost impossible to fly external loads.

For lumber, two ropes were tied to the base of the fore and aft float struts. Boards were stacked on top of the ropes on each float, the longest on the bottom. Weight of the increasing load was judged by the water line of the pontoon. Lastly, the ropes were wrapped around the outside of the pile and pulled tight behind each float strut and secured. Most important, a second rope was strung between the first two ropes and cinched tight. This method pulled the front and rear ropes together, using mechanical advantage. The resultant harness was very taut. The plane was spun around at the dock in order to load each float. This could not be accomplished in high winds, nor would it be wise to haul lumber in turbulent conditions.

Propane cylinders were usually moved with the Beaver. Using planks, five cylinders could be rolled into the cargo area and stacked horizontally. This procedure required a rugged pilot, because each tank weighed about 150 pounds. Many float plane pilots ended up lame, from lifting under cramped conditions. After the interior cylinders were in place, two additional tanks were lashed to each float. We used to fly with the rear doors cracked open for fume ventilation. A door ajar a couple of inches will evacuate a huge volume of air once airborne.

Freezers, refrigerators, generators, and other heavy, bulky items could be moved on top of a float. Ropes were arranged in a similar fashion as that described for lumber. Also, any convenient attachment point was secured for good measure. The old Beaver looked comical flying along with a big box freezer extending from one side.

Picture windows presented a special challenge. The last thing you needed was for one to shatter on takeoff or in flight. The trick was to invent a way to place the window inside. Often, by removing the front passenger door, the front passenger seat, and the rear seat, a decent-sized frame could be squeezed in. The load would be roped to interior cargo rings. The plane flew well without the door.

The external load that generated the most profit was the canoe. With the designation by the federal government of the Allagash River as a wild, protected stream, demand escalated from canoeists for transportation. The most practical way to reach both ends of the Allagash was by plane. The Beaver made most trips because it could easily haul two canoes and four passengers plus luggage. The canoes were lashed just like a pile of lumber, but an additional short rope held the bow. The adventurers were dropped off at Churchill Dam and picked up in the St. Francis River.

When Beth and I bought Hardscrabble, we had to settle for a smaller floatplane. I continued to move tons of freight, but more trips were required than at Folsom's. Most cargo was kitchen staples—case after case of canned vegetables, pie fillings, flour, sugar, etc. We started making trips in the late winter when daytime temperatures were regularly above freezing. Items easily damaged by cold nights were stored in the root cellar.

In late winter, Spencer Lake would still have thick ice everywhere except the last 100 feet before the shoreline. This was because the melting snow raised the lake level and created open water. The method we found most efficient was to stop the plane 500 feet from shore and load the staples into a 14 foot boat. We'd push the boat over the slick ice, ready to jump aboard when the bow broke through. Usually the boat had enough momentum to coast to the beach, so we could unload. Once I got a sudden surprise. Pushing on the stern, I stepped into an ice-fishing hole that had been enlarged by the melt. In an instant, I was holding onto the boat, submerged to my armpits. The shock was so great that I struggled for breath. With a helping hand from Carl, I popped back up on the ice. Fortunately, a warm cabin was nearby.

Obviously, these all-day hauling episodes required a big crew. In addition to a pilot, loaders in town and unloaders at Hardscrabble were necessary. Our friends always volunteered for the task, and a party atmosphere was the norm. Once the ice melted we moved more perishable goods by floatplane. That exercise seemed a breeze, compared to the earlier efforts.

Hunting trophies always rode on the floats. A slice was made in the hide behind the tough sinew at the deer's knee, enabling the rope to pass through. With the knees secured high on the float struts, the animal could not move. During November, the air was often well below freezing while the water temperature was above 32. As a result, ice formed over the surface of the floats on every takeoff. The deer blood, frozen into that ice, colored the floats red during the season.

The squeamish reader may want to end the chapter here.

People died and were killed in the woods. Sometimes the only way to evacuate the body was by floatplane. A medical examiner was flown in and accompanied the body out. During hunting season, heart attacks claimed some sports. On occasion, several days went by before the body was found. If the temperature was low enough, the deceased was frozen rock-solid, often into an unnatural shape. The only possible way to move such a body by floatplane was tied to a float.

Dick Folsom told a story that occurred before I was hired. One busy Saturday, the pilots were busy flying hunters and their trophies. A small crowd had gathered around the docks to admire some of the larger deer. By coincidence, Dick had been asked to fly a frozen body. As he flew above town 1000 feet high, several people noticed the unusually large buck tied to the floats. Soon the crowd swelled. When he landed and taxied toward the dock people began to scatter. Dick said some were literally running away! Some folks may enjoy watching horror movies, but no one likes to feel like they're in one!

CHAPTER 9

◇◇◇

Fear of the Woods

Almost all of our hunters were quick to express trepidation about venturing into the huge woodland that surrounded Hardscrabble. That was natural. Their home turf was totally unlike the woods of northern Maine. Most were accustomed to small patches of forest surrounded by farm fields, with familiar trails crossing wood lots that led to hunting stands, used for decades. Burt Packard (an old friend and master Maine Guide who we hired each fall) and I quickly realized that in order to make our guests comfortable, it was essential to have an orientation on the first Sunday of each week—a non-hunting day, by law, in Maine.

We divided the session into two parts. The first event was a firearms check, followed by a refresher course in compass navigation. Being careful not to embarrass anyone, we placed a series of 10-inch-diameter paper plates 75 yards away on the firing range. Also, Burt explained that due to rough handling during transport to Maine, it was not uncommon to find rifles off target upon arrival. Watching carefully, it was an easy matter to separate competent from inexperienced marksmen. The crack shots loaded the gun effortlessly, stepped up, and shot the center out of the plate. In the other group, some could not remember how to insert the ammunition clip into the rifle, or flinched so badly anticipating the recoil, that the bullet missed the plate. At least we knew who to watch out for and assist. After target practice, we practiced walking compass lines, first in the camp field, then in open forest, and finally in dense undergrowth. By the end of orientation it was easy to sense how relieved some of the sports felt.

The secret of hunting success lies in finding where deer are living. Without limiting boundaries, groups of does roam over a large area. During November, bucks traveled constantly from group to group in an attempt to mate. The bottom line is that if the hunter fails to cover a lot of forest, chances of success are minimal. For selfish reasons, we needed our guests to be successful. But how do you encourage a hunter to venture out?

We devised two schemes that worked. The first was possible given the nearby topography—several glacial ponds and ridges surrounding Spencer Lake—within three miles of the shore. This feature made it possible to fly hunters into ponds in the morning that were within easy walking distance to the lodge. The return trip headed gradually downhill, and never changed direction. Since the lake was three miles long, it was almost impossible to miss the mark. In the late afternoon, Burt or I would cruise the shoreline in boats picking up arrivals.

Some of the guests were just not comfortable left on their own. Either Burt or I would accompany this bunch. The group would spread out in a line, separated by sight distance, and everyone was carefully instructed which compass course to walk. We gave each hunter two compasses that attached to his coat. Hunting on foot required very slow forward progress and constant vigilance. We took just a few steps at a time, then stood for a minute or two. All were trained to check their compass every time we stopped. They did this by looking ahead and identifying a distant tree, and then walking toward it every time we moved. Most sports were amazed by the swath of land covered by lunch. The return pace was more rapid. The deadline to be home was 3:30 pm.

Some readers may be wondering what happens when a deer is killed. Once the animal is located, the first rule is that everyone unloads. From this point on, guns were passed around as the men "spelled" each other, so it was essential to be safe. Sometimes, the successful hunter volunteered to field-dress the trophy, but most indicated that it was their first time. Either Burt or I performed the chore and explained the procedure. Gutting a deer required a sharp slim knife and considerable patience. The goal was to carefully slice the belly skin in order to expose the internal organs without cutting into the innards. Proper execution results in very little mess. The insides are removed as one long piece and left in the woods, a tasty treat for scavengers. After that, we decided whether to drag the buck uphill to a pond or downhill all the way to the lake. I flew many animals from one of the ponds to the lake. Their spines were placed on top of the float, legs lashed to the float strut.

Next, a smooth-barked hardwood sapling, about one and one-half inches in diameter was harvested. The fastest way to accomplish this was to shoot a small tree with a shotgun. Two properly placed shots yielded a piece three feet long. The center of this handle was tied to one end of a rope while the other end was tied to the base of the antlers, so as to make a dragging harness four feet long.

Most guests were not athletes, and some were well out of shape. Therefore, the secret of a long drag was for all to take very short turns, two at a time. Fifteen-second shifts worked well. So with many exchanges of guns and coats, you headed for home. One of our drags lasted about six hours! An animal shot late in the day stayed in the woods overnight, suspended from a tree limb.

In the end, hunting in a remote area was challenging—all the better to provide our guests with an enduring experience of great satisfaction from surviving the ordeal. Stories about long, tedious drags were repeated over and over. And any sport who banished the fear of the forest felt an even greater sense of accomplishment.

CHAPTER 10

◇◇◇

Trophy Dreams

Hunters fantasize about shooting the "buck of a lifetime." Most, of course, never do! Huge deer are usually middle-aged specimens, and they survive four or five years by a combination of luck and stealth. During my entire hunting career, I have only been fortunate to see a few. The game camera on my farm captures pictures of trophy stags, but the recorded time is usually in the wee hours of the morning.

Some of our sports came to Hardscrabble with only one goal: harvest a behemoth. Most of these men lived in states with huge populations of smaller deer. To just shoot a deer was old hat. Essentially, they came chasing a dream.

One such dreamer was a wildlife biologist from New Jersey who had booked a hunt at the Philadelphia Sportsmen Show. Carl and I knew from our brief conversation at the expo that Keith knew deer and he liked to hunt alone. After breakfast, on a Monday in early November, Keith pulled out a topographical map and pointed to a location.

"I'd like to hunt in this area," he said.

"Well…that ridge is about five to six hundred feet above the lodge and over an hour away on foot," I cautioned.

"Don't worry," Keith said, "I walk in the woods for a living."

That night, after a full day on Hedgehog Mountain, he gave me a summary.

"Lots of small deer, but no fresh tracks of a large buck. However, there were old tracks of a heavy animal. I'm going back tomorrow."

The plateau that held the herd was much closer to Little Enchanted Pond than to the lodge. After being flown into the pond the next morning, Keith arrived quickly at the chosen spot. On Tuesday, no change. Wednesday produced a cruising set of heavy prints, but no sighting.

Thursday dawned with drizzle and fog. Flying was out of the question. Keith took off anyway. At 2:30 pm, he walked into the camp yard with dried blood on his hands and a broad smile on his face.

"How big is he?" I asked.

"The rack is twelve points and perfectly symmetrical. I can't budge him," Keith replied.

"There isn't enough daylight left to return to the scene today," I said. "We'll hope for the best. If coyotes find a dead deer, little will remain after a couple days, but we'll probably get back to it in time."

Friday morning, six men volunteered to drag. I doubt they knew what was in store. After an hour hike we arrived. I stared at the trophy. The animal was untouched and huge!

"Keith, I know you study deer for a living, so you must realize that this is one in ten thousand. My guess is 220–230 pounds dressed. That in itself makes him special. But Keith, that rack is the most perfect I've ever seen. The symmetry is uncanny. You've got bragging rights for the rest of your life!"

The drag was downhill to Spencer Lake. Each pair of men dragged 15- to 30-second shifts. Four hours later, everyone was admiring a "once-in-a-lifetime buck," hanging from the game pole.

In December, a package arrived at the post office. Inside was a hand-carved decoy from Keith, inscribed, "To my good friend Jake—1978." That remembrance sits on my desk.

The only other hint of a memorable buck was seen in probably the most popular hunting area—Bear Mountain, west of the lake. For the first two weeks of the season, before the small ponds iced over, I landed hunters in Beck Pond near the summit of the ridge. The walk back to Spencer Lake was two miles in length, descending gradually through huge, mature hardwood growth. Nut trees abounded. Sometimes visibility was 100 yards. Mixed in with the hardwood were frequent "black nubbles," that provided hiding places for deer.

For two seasons many hunters chased the "monster buck of Bear Mountain." His hoof prints were distinctive. In addition to the size, one appeared to be deformed. Instead of coming to a point in the front, the impression in the snow was rectangular. Numerous guests claimed to have seen a flash of the stag. No one fired a shot in two years. Score: trophy deer—one, guests—one.

Maine has a relatively small population, and word of unusual events spreads rapidly. Truck drivers carrying logs motor the same route to the mill every day and stop in the same stores for snacks. Gossip travels along the highway. Word reached Greenville that a man from Farmington, Maine, named Titcomb had shot a record buck. On a hunch, I guessed it could be the caretaker of a private lodge located about a mile west of Beck Pond.

On the phone, Mr. Titcomb confirmed that he was the lucky man. Then he added, "Jake, I'm having the whole animal mounted. Come over in March for a look."

That spring I took him up on the invite. The caretaker made maple syrup and first thing, insisted I try a small glass of his effort. Nothing beats fresh, warm maple syrup. Then he led me to the prize. That buck dwarfed Keith's. And sure enough, the right front foot was turned under permanently. The buck walked on the wrist of its foot.

One less trophy to dream about…

CHAPTER 11

◇◇◇

"Brace Both Arms on the Back of My Seat!"

The majority of people who pay to tour a Sportsmen Show fall into one of two categories. The first is families—a significant percentage of the whole. What better way to entertain rural kids than to: view booth after booth filled with exotic taxidermy, fish at the children's trout pool, buy several doughboys, and sit back and watch the twice-daily show. The shows were often hosted by sports celebrities, and featured both dramatic high-wire stunts and events such as tame-bear wrestling. The second group of folks that filed by actually hunted or fished. Logo baseball caps, jacket patches, and a bag full of brochures were the trademarks of this latter group. Often they appeared in groups.

So when an impeccably dressed, middle-aged couple came along, I took note. I watched the trim man, dressed in a three-piece suit and camel-hair overcoat, slowly walk by several other booths. He then squared himself in front of the Hardscrabble counter and stared at the large color photo of Spencer Lake hanging in the rear of the display. Finally, he placed a business card before me, which indicated he was the CEO of a steel company, and said, "I grew up on Spencer Lake. My father ran the camps during the twenties, thirties, and into the beginning of World War II."

I was thrilled to meet him, and learned one fact after another about the history of Gerard, Maine, as it was called at that time. One story stood out. He detailed how one morning he heard a noise like nothing he had experienced before. What originally sounded similar to distant thunder, grew to a low, continuous rumble, and became louder and louder. A very large, green, multi-engine flying boat appeared at the far end of Spencer Lake, three miles away. The behemoth flew directly over the camps. The plane was so low, heads were easily visible in the side windows. Five minutes later it reappeared, made a lazy circle at the far end of the pond, and set up to land. After touchdown, the pilot approached the beach in front of the lodge and moored the amphibian. Numerous military officers deplaned and came ashore in a rubber boat.

The brass stated that they needed to look around, but refused to divulge why. Everyone disappeared up the buckboard trail, and the group was gone for several hours. When the party returned, they were pleasant, but yielded no further clues. The plane blasted off.

Within weeks, the reason for the scouting trip became obvious. A location two miles north of Gerard had been selected as the future site of a German prisoner-of-war camp. Buildings were constructed by military crews with the help of the local paper company, which owned the land. A new road was bulldozed to the camp. The incoming prisoners would work as loggers, cutting four-foot pulp. Each prisoner was required to fell, buck, and stack one and one-half cords of wood each day—a lot of hard work! At that time, the forest was harvested with axes and hand saws. Many local residents found work supervising the cutters.

After the war, the collection of buildings was abandoned. Occasionally, woodworkers stayed for a season, but gradually the structures deteriorated. Years later, two trappers, Bob Wagg and Walter Lane, adopted what was left of the prisoner camp. Both men were rough around the edges, as remote trappers tend to be, and soon their new home became a remote place to party for some of the local men and women. A wonderful documentary film, titled "Dead River Rough Cut," was produced, detailing the life of these two characters. Eventually, the landowner became unhappy with the antics of the trappers and friends. The company burned the buildings. Wagg did not want to abandon his old haunts, so he moved into a cabin about 25 miles away. He continued to trap.

Coincidentally, a short time after that trade show, the old woodsman became aware that we had restored Spencer Lake Camps. He traveled in an old, beat-up woods vehicle, and often appeared at Hardscrabble late in the day. I enjoyed talking with Bob, and the guests could not get enough of his entertaining yarns. Many of the sports treated Bob to beers (one objective of his visit).

One day, after entertaining the guests for a while, Bob approached me.

"Jake, I'll pay you whatever you want for a ride over the lake. For years, I've had dreams about looking down on Spencer. It's like I'm a bird and can go anywhere I want."

"Bob, you're not paying me a cent. Don't even think of arguing. Now let's go."

Off we went. Even though Bob had crisscrossed the land below us countless times, he became disoriented when in the air.

"Bob, off the right wingtip is Whipple Pond."

"Bullshit, Whipple is long and narrow. What the hell's got into your head?"

"Bob, I'm not bullshitting you, that is Whipple Pond! I've landed there many times. It just looks different from 500 feet high."

I had experienced this phenomenon with passengers new to flight many times. Some people cannot look at the landscape below as you would a map. Instead they think in ground distances and lefts and rights. Nothing appears to make sense below. In time, Bob adapted and was actually pointing out small features on the ground not easily visible from above.

Bob talked nonstop for a while, and then said less and less. I assumed he was lost in his "bird dream." Suddenly, total silence; the engine had quit! No pond was within gliding distance. My only alternative was to land into the wind in the forest canopy, flying as slowly as possible. I turned around and started to say, "Bob, brace both arms on the back of my seat," but quickly saw he was taking a little snooze. His elbow was pinned against the rear throttle, pushing the control all the way to idle.

"Bob!" I yelled, no response.

We were descending straight down.

I slapped the side of his head.

"Huh? What?" Bob said, jerking awake.

That did the trick. The engine roared to life, and we turned toward Hardscrabble.

CHAPTER 12

◇◇◇

Two Little Pigs

During our first season, Beth and I met two farmers at the Boxborough Sportsman Show who were devoted fly fishermen. Both were jovial men, full of "get up and go." For many seasons they visited Hardscrabble during the same week, and we always looked forward to their arrival. Perhaps they enjoyed our company as well, because each year, while at the show, we were invited to share an evening meal at one of their homes.

Over supper during the second season, one of the men made an offer.

"How'd you like a pair of piglets? We can deliver them next spring."

Beth and I looked at each other.

"Sure," I said.

"I'll put them in a cat-carrying box so they'll survive the plane trip to Hardscrabble with Folsom's."

Early in May, Thea and Zeke helped create a spacious pen and shelter for the new arrivals.

The little critters were none the worse for wear after the thirteen hour drive from Pennsylvania to Greenville. The two lively, vocal pigs were a hit at the Air Service. Weighing just a couple of pounds each, with soft hair, fellow passengers found them irresistible. Everyone had to cuddle a piglet.

After an uneventful flight, Thea carried the box to the pen, and the porkers were released. The animals would be under the care of Thea and Zeke, and both took the responsibility seriously. We started a tradition of naming our new critters for members of Folsom's crew. This pair were called Dick and Connie, after the founder and radio operator. They were fed a grain starter during the first couple of weeks, but soon Connie and Dick thrived on leftovers. At the end of each meal, a bucket of waste waited for the pigs' enjoyment. Zeke or Thea would carry the bucket to the pen and dump the contents into an old steel sink.

Pigs gain weight rapidly, and soon their diet expanded. Zeke loved to fish in the narrows for small chubs. In a short time he could fill a bucket. One day he threw a chub into the pen. The fish, which was flipping around, immediately caught the attention of the pigs. It was quickly killed and eaten. After that, Zeke emptied half a bucket each day. Interestingly, the pigs killed all of the fish before eating the first one.

As summer wore on, the animals ceased to be cute. Nearly mature, Connie and Dick were no longer novel. The kids had to be regularly reminded to tend to their chores. During September and October, the slow season, Beth and our children returned to Greenville so Thea and Zeke could attend the opening of school. (They returned in November.) I became the pig-feeder and added grain to their diet to replace the kitchen scraps and chubs.

Burt and I killed and processed our meat in late October. We had to employ methods possible in a remote location. Hardscrabble's 1953 Super C Farmall tractor, with loader, made the task much easier. First, we parked the machine, with the bucket raised above the feeding trough, for several days to acclimate the critters. Then, on the appointed day, we filled the old sink with fresh grain and waited as Connie and Dick gorged themselves. I slipped a noose onto a hind leg of each animal and attached the other ends to the bucket. Burt started the tractor and on my signal, raised the bucket rapidly. Almost instantly, both were upside down at chest height. They were quickly dispatched and bled out, and the real work began.

First the innards were removed in the normal fashion; next, the carcasses were dipped in the mountain stream next to camp in order to cleanse the meat. The Super C made this easy. We could position the tractor's front wheels next to the edge of the wharf and dip repeatedly. During this phase one year we had a unique experience.

Burt was a huge man with a beard and lots of hair. I had a beard at the time, and we both were unkempt, having lived in the woods for months. Each time we dipped, a plume of red flowed down the stream. Suddenly, we looked up and saw a young couple carrying backpacks about a quarter mile away, approaching up the shoreline. We were 18 miles into the woods; no one ever arrived on foot. We watched intently. When they got close enough to make out the details of our operation they came to an abrupt halt. The girl emitted a loud scream and both ran away. We called out but they did not stop, and we never saw them again.

Another step in pork preparation was dealing with the pig hair—not easily removed. In order to do so at all, it had to be scalded by water heated to about 160 degrees F. We built a fire under a 55-gallon drum, and when the water was ready, dipped a pig briefly. Grudgingly, the hair fell out or could be scraped off. Extra time spent at this stage ensured the hams would not have nicked skins.

Since we favored two hams, two sides of bacon, and two racks of pork chops from each animal, we cut accordingly. Butchering was time-consuming if done carefully. After several hours, the chore was finished. Then the hams and bacon had to be cured with salt and smoke.

Salt was rubbed over the surface, and cuts were made to expose the deep bones. Using our fingers, salt was forced into the slices and worked around the bone. Next, the meat was brined in a bucket overnight.

The following morning, the camp smoker was stoked with apple wood and set ablaze. Smokers are designed so that only smoke reaches the meat chamber, and the temperature inside remains cool. Smoking can be used for either preservation or to enhance flavor, depending on duration. Since our meat was refrigerated, only two days was necessary.

I flew the final product home to Greenville, where some was frozen and some refrigerated. We swore that the pigs we raised tasted better than commercial pork. Thus started a yearly tradition that put meat in our freezer every fall.

Young couple, if you should read this…now you know.

CHAPTER 13

◇◇◇

Beth Seduces Deer

Realizing how many hours Beth spent over the stove, Burt and I encouraged her to take off a couple of hours in the early afternoons to hunt. We spotted several locations within a 15-minute walk of the kitchen, where elevations offered great views of small hardwood saddles. These small cuts through the ridges were favored traveling routes for deer. On sunny days, Beth could stand, protected from the wind and warmed by the sunlight. Almost always, nothing passed by during the short time she was free. On two occasions, there was cause for major adrenaline rushes.

On a bright day with a stiff west wind, Burt and I chose to hunt by moving very slowly into the wind perpendicular to the western shore of Spencer Lake. We planned to spend the entire day covering no more than a mile. One of Beth's favorite perches would be behind us by noontime. We suggested that she select that spot with the hope that any deer which had evaded us might pass that way. This is the experience she related to us:

"I couldn't feel the brisk breeze because of the eight-foot wall of rock directly behind me. I was resting against the backdrop, watching the ravine. Suddenly, small rocks were raining down on me. Two hoofs came into view from above, followed by two more. A large buck landed just ten feet away, directly in front of the bluff. The animal had leapt from the top of the rock! Slowly, the trophy turned its head and stared directly at me. The beast was giant. It took a step toward me. I was paralyzed, could barely breathe, much less raise the Model 92 Winchester. In a flash, after two huge bounds, the antlers disappeared. I was shaking and couldn't stop."

That evening, the sports ribbed Beth for not shooting a stag ten feet away.

"I'm sorry; I'm sorry for not filling the freezer," Beth said over and over.

The second incident occurred later in the season. I had returned to the lodge early to split firewood. Beth, now armed with a single-shot shotgun, decided to try one last time. She told me that she would be in a small hardwood saddle to the east, above the lodge.

Splitting firewood is always a chore, but on cold days the task warms the body and does not seem as onerous as in the summer. After swinging the splitting maul for a few hours your mind easily drifts to another place.

Coming to, I heard crying. Beth was approaching, hysterical, tears streaming down her face. I ran to meet her expecting some kind of injury.

"Jake, Jake, I hurt him! I can't stand it! That beautiful deer walked right toward me, nose in the air. I shot when we were 100 feet apart. He looked right at me after I fired and bleated like a lamb. Blood was running out of his mouth. But damn it, he kept looking at me. That's it, I'm done hunting!"

"Bethy, calm down. You didn't do anything wrong. I'm sure the buck walked a few steps out of sight and fell over. You're sure you were in the Hardscrabble saddle?"

"Yes, right where you walked with me. Jake, I feel sick!"

"Bethy, don't worry; I'll go find the buck. You need to get supper ready."

Just a few hours of daylight remained. I grabbed my 35 Remington and hurried toward the spot. Beth headed toward the kitchen.

Once near the valley, I slowed to a crawl. The deer smelled me before I saw him, and whirled. I fired quickly, but probably missed.

I could tell by the stag's gait that Beth had inflicted a serious wound. For more than an hour I followed the blood trail on the snow. Several times the animal spotted me from a distance and limped away. Finally, I saw the antlers on top of a small hummock. Probably extremely weakened, the trophy was watching the wrong direction. One shot finished the hunt.

I had no idea how far the deer lay from the Hardscrabble four-wheel drive road, but daylight was fading. After quickly gutting Beth's first kill, I took off on a compass course. What a surprise when the road materialized within 300 feet.

After hiking back to camp and returning with our 1953 Willys Jeep, one of the sports helped me drag the heavy carcass to the road. We were drinking a beer just after dark. Beth had filled the freezer.

Beth's trophy weighed over 200 pounds without its innards. We carefully caped the animal and hired a taxidermist to craft a full-running mount for our display booth. Over the years many Sportsman Show visitors admired the final result.

CHAPTER 14

◇◇◇

Scientists Like to Look Down

Before Google Maps and ESRI, the only easily obtainable aerial photographs came from the United States Department of Agriculture. The photos were expensive, and shipping was very slow. Also, black and white was the only option. As a result, foresters, geologists, biologists, and planners relied on floatplane flights to gather up-to-date information. Coloration of the trees, land, and water was important to these professionals.

At Folsom's Air Service, I enjoyed many flight hours watching scientists work. Later, during the Hardscrabble years, my Supercub was in demand as a study platform. The Cubs have fore and aft seating and are high wing, so left and right downward visibility is excellent. Also, the slow-speed wing allows rock-solid flights at 60 miles an hour.

Eagle nest surveys were conducted early in the spring. At that time, eagles were an endangered species. The Fish and Wildlife folks had a map of every known eagle nest in Maine. We flew from nest to nest looking for surviving chicks. Care was taken to not harass the birds. An occasional high point of a trip was a sighting of an unmapped nest. By comparing data year to year, the gradual recovery of the majestic bird was chronicled.

A different set of biologists counted black ducks, in order to set federal bag limits. We flew low over coastal waters, estimating flock sizes in the numerous coves. As we looked down, we often saw hundreds of ducks clustered. The men and women had years of experience and were accomplished guessers. Periodically, they would snap aerial photographs as a control measure. By comparing the estimate to a photo count, they became better and better at judging the populations. Sometimes we were airborne for four and a half hours at a time.

Deer census was done in the winter. In northern Maine, deer "yard" most of the winter. Large numbers gather at the same location year after year. As the snow depth increases, they pack down a series of trails beneath the thick forest canopy. By overflying the "deer yards," the biologist counted actual animal sightings, and used a formula to estimate the total population. Later, he or she snowshoed into several yards to double-check the result. During the Hardscrabble years, the deer population plummeted, due to predation and a series of harsh winters. Once we found an empty yard that had previously held 150 animals. My first thought was: how can it ever come back? If all the deer in an extensive area are dead, how long will it take for wanderers to repopulate?

Snow surveys were necessary to prevent spring flooding on dam-controlled rivers. Yearly data went back to 1900. Sample locations were selected under hardwood growth and near ponds in the headwaters of the river. We landed on skis and snowshoed to the test site. A hollow tube was lowered through the snow to the ground, in order to measure depth. The snow and tube were weighed on a scale. Water content, measured in inches of rain, was calculated. The dams' gates were then adjusted to reach a lake level low enough to make room for the spring snowmelt. Sampling all of the locations took several days.

Another experience with assisting scientists related to the devastation of fir trees in Maine from the spruce budworm. The insect is cyclical on forty-year intervals. In order to determine an aerial spraying schedule, entomologists snipped small boughs from treetops all over northern Maine. I usually landed on a pond and beached the plane. The sample was taken using a set of shears with a 30-foot, screw-together handle. The boughs fell to the ground and were placed in labeled polyethylene bags. The stage of metamorphosis was determined later in a lab. This saga went on for weeks.

Meanwhile, foresters flew just above the treetops, estimating tree mortality. Using maps overlaid with grids, they wrote a death percentage in each box as I passed over. This task was only possible on low-wind days.

Foresters also flew over townships to determine the mix of tree or arbor species. In Maine, timberland is taxed based on the type and age of forest growth. Over time we discovered remote tracts where existing records were dead wrong. As technology advanced, the timber companies hired aerial photographers to record the forest, with film sensitive to different wavelengths of the spectrum. These were similar to infrared shots. The prints exhibited a mix of vivid colors: purple, orange, magenta. The hypothesis was that different tree species could be recognized by color. It worked.

Geologists are a different breed. Most scientific people we flew loved to describe their work, and accordingly, I learned a lot. But since the rock crowd was searching for valuable minerals, they were tight-lipped. Watching carefully, you could deduce quite a bit. They utilized similar photographs to those of the foresters. The plan was to fly over known deposits and scrutinize the depiction on the print. The theory was that trees sucked up water rich in the underlying mineral and showed up as a certain distinctive shade. Because they hardly ever spoke, I don't know the outcome.

Occasionally, unusual events prompted flights. If a suspected tornado had hit the forest, the fact was confirmed from the air. Likewise, algae blooms were distinctive by shades of green. Sometimes a careless logging operation sent plumes of brown silt into a pond. If a severe windstorm ruined huge volumes of valuable timber, the paper companies were anxious to quantify their loss.

The most unusual naturalist was the "turtle man." A recluse who trapped the reptiles and controlled the snapping turtle market in the Northeast, Zeke delivered wet burlap bags full of snappers to the best restaurants in Boston and New York. When we flew, he never said a word. Finger commands replaced talk—go right, go left—and had to be seen, rather than heard. Since I flew over this terrain day after day, I knew exactly where we were the entire time. We often crossed a bog, then re-crossed it later, but he never asked me to circle the water body. I was certain that Zeke did not want to telegraph his interest. Perhaps he was not eager to divulge where he caught the beasts.

I'm glad for the opportunity of piloting those flights. By watching and listening to highly trained professionals, I got an adult education on the environment where I coexisted with plants and fauna. Many times I read newspaper articles based on the data assembled from my plane. Increasingly, I became more aware of the fragility of our world.

CHAPTER 15

◇◇◇

Can My Dog Come?

At the Suffern, New York Sportsman Show, Beth and I, almost simultaneously, noticed a giant of a man heading up our aisle. Since ninety-nine percent of time spent at a show is boring, we tended to make small talk about unusual people who strolled by the booth.

"Beth, he must weigh well over 300 pounds and stand six inches above me." "I bet he is all of six foot six."

"Jake, do me a favor. Don't insult him! Oh guess what, he's headed right toward us."

"Sir, may I help you?" I asked.

"You betcha. Hardscrabble has been highly recommended to me by a close friend who fishes all over the country. Do you remember Hal Webber?"

"I certainly do. If we didn't observe a catch-and-release rule, Hal would have cleaned out the trout ponds."

"I'm a chef at One Foreside in New York. I get two weeks' vacation, but the deadline for locking in dates is next week. Do you have space for the first week in June?"

"Let's take a peek at the book. I think so. Yep, one cabin is available from June first through the tenth."

"Sign me up. Will two hundred dollars hold the reservation? That's all I brought."

"No problem."

"Oh...before I fork over the money, the most important question of all. Is my dog welcome?"

No guest had ever made a similar request. We spent at least ten minutes talking about his Saint Bernard. He stated that the animal was professionally trained, loved people, and had spent hours lying in the bow of a boat, watching him fish. I asked how the dog might react to the airplane flights, and he assured me that the pet would remain totally calm and silent. I mentioned that I might or might not always be able to carry both of them at once. Would the Saint Bernard be comfortable flying without him? Jerry was confident that all would go well. We finally agreed to the proposal with the understanding that should the dog present a problem, Jerry would leave, and I would issue a partial refund. Lodge owners tend to be flexible when they really need income!

Rufus, the huge beast, behaved perfectly on the flight in with Folsom's. Max, the pilot, indicated that he had quickly made friends with numerous other passengers at the air service. He was a beautiful, well-mannered animal, and must have weighed well over one hundred pounds.

Early the next morning was the first test. We walked down toward the dock, and Jerry repeatedly told Rufus that it was time to take an airplane ride. I swear the dog shook his head and appeared to understand. At the dock, Jerry scooped his pet up with both arms and placed the animal in the baggage area behind the rear seat. The two of us then climbed into our seats. I could tell by the waterline level along the pontoons that the Supercub was heavily loaded. However, the large, high-lift wing and powerful engine were more than ample for the task. The plane broke the water quickly, and soon we were landing at Little Enchanted Pond. This routine was going to work after all! Jerry and Rufus enjoyed a day of great dry-fly fishing.

Near the end of the week, Jerry wanted to try the same pond again. No problem. The guests had lost a couple days of fishing mid-week due to persistent electrical storms. So on Friday, the three of us repeated the flight to Little Enchanted.

When the plane was secured to shore, Jerry placed Rufus on land and followed. After one step the dog froze; his hair stood on end. He emitted a low, persistent growl. Rufus acted like he'd become a statue.

"Jerry, there must be a moose or bear handy."

"I don't think that is the problem. He's had extensive training to not react to horses or other dogs. Rufus, what's wrong, buddy?"

Jerry's third or fourth step told the story. The ground ahead erupted with plumes of smoke and small torches of fire. Lightning had struck a tree and ignited the top ground cover—an area composed of boulders surrounded by organic decay.

"Back to the plane," I hollered.

We beat a hasty retreat and flew back to Camp. Forest fires are a great worry if your business is surrounded by wild land. An out-of-control blaze could consume your lodge very quickly. I called the Maine Forest Service and four-wheel-drive trucks carrying fire pumps were dispatched almost immediately.

Upon arrival, a ranger ran up to me. "Can you fly me and a pump to Little Enchanted?"

"Absolutely," I said.

After landing, he quickly screwed a suction hose onto the pump inlet, then a coil of firehose onto the outlet. The gasoline engine roared to life on the first pull. Soon a torrent of water was directed toward the fire. The blaze had burned so deeply into the ground that steam rose for hours from the rocks.

Several weeks later, Rufus received a framed certificate of appreciation and a new one-dollar bill from the Maine Forest Service.

As a side note, Jerry showed Beth one cooking trick after another. One technique, which she still uses, involves repeatedly basting a turkey with maple syrup or honey as it roasts. The result is a dark brown, crunchy skin while the moisture is sealed within the bird. Delicious!

CHAPTER 16

◇◇◇

Headlights in the Pines

Hardscrabble Lodge was situated in a wonderfully protected narrow valley. Ridges to the east and west, in addition to the mountain in the rear, blocked cold winds. The southern exposure warmed the land.

When temperatures in Maine finally climbed after the long winter, the melt around the camp yard was weeks ahead of the surrounding forest. Grass showed hints of green when two feet of snow still blocked parts of the access road and 18 inches of ice remained on the lake.

A fellow lodge-owner, Jerry, and I often took advantage of that quirk of location and flew in by floatplane to spend a few days relaxing before spring and tinkering on outside camp repairs. The flight was possible because Jerry's camps were located at a river outlet, and Hardscrabble was next to a narrows, both of which thawed very early.

We liked the feeling of peace and nearly total silence upon arrival. After all, no other human was located within 20 miles. It was easy to settle into a routine that revolved around cooking and eating three great meals, mixed with the occasional chore. Up at daylight and in the sack by dark.

An extremely sound sleeper, I was very slow to become aware of someone shaking me. After another couple of seconds, Jerry materialized as the shaker.

"Get up, get up!" he hoarsely whispered.

Nothing made sense. Although deep in the night and pitch dark, a diffuse light was shining through the cabin window.

Jerry said softly, "Someone is here; look out the rear window."

My brain was not processing. No one else could be here because no one else could get here. That was one reason Jerry and I made the trip.

After standing, I saw two truck headlights shining from the edge of the woods where the road emerged. Men were moving near the vehicle. The bright beams obscured the details in the shadows to the rear of the vehicle, but both bodies moved in unison. Neither intruder approached the camp.

We both had slept in union suits, one-piece garments of long underwear usually colored red. In a chilly camp it was usually everyone's habit to wear the things day and night. The next thing I realized, Jerry was racing for the door, grabbing an axe next to it, and jumping into a set of boots. I followed but was only able to find a shovel for a weapon. We had no plan and moved fueled by adrenalin and motivated to protect our turf. Jerry set the pace—a dead run to the woods.

Arriving at the truck, we totally surprised the men. Jerry held the axe overhead and lunged close to the larger man, lowering the blade to face level.

"What the hell do you think you're doing? Don't take another step!" he yelled.

The guy was startled. "Hey, sorry…ah…uh…easy, man…"

Both men held their arms overhead. Each wore a green, checkered wool coat and felt hat. I also noticed that both had "Scott Paper issue" red rubber boots.

"Why the hell are you two here in the middle of the night?"

"When we got to camp and tried to light the range, the cylinder was empty. We were just borrowing a tank which we planned to replace next week."

"Where is your camp?" I asked.

"Five miles north."

"Jake, these two are blowing smoke through their assholes! Look in the bed of the truck! Count them: one, two, three, four, FIVE cylinders! Now why do you need five tanks to cook breakfast?"

No answer.

"I've heard enough of your bullshit," Jerry yelled, approaching the duo. "Unload all five bottles now or your dead asses will end up in the Somerset jail!"

The men shot a glance at each other, and without protest, immediately did as Jerry ordered. The tanks weighed 150 pounds, so they had to strain pretty hard. The larger of the two was obviously muscular, and that concerned me!

After our property was returned, I asked, "How the hell did you drive in here through all the snow?"

Both pointed to the huge tires mounted on the pickup. Neither Jerry nor I had ever seen anything similar. Each was easily twice the diameter of normal rubber. Apparently, a tire that size could negotiate two feet of snow.

"Now," Jerry admonished, "turn that piece of junk around and never come back! And one last question: if you are a thief, why did you pay for a Maine plate that says Suzie?"

Without saying another word, they left. Thank God for Jerry!

Before we went back to sleep, I said, "One of their faces looked familiar."

The next morning, after another huge breakfast, Jerry said, "Let's walk out along their tracks to find out how the hell those tires work in this much snow; I'm curious."

Only a short distance into the pine forest, he stopped suddenly. "Look!"

There, not 100 feet from the pile of propane cylinders, and behind a large Norway pine tree, was a set of men's tracks. Another person had hidden while we confronted the other two. Simultaneously, we shared the same thought: How lucky we were! If the third man had approached, we would have been doomed.

Two weeks later, the identity of the younger man's face clicked. I had seen him years before. Then a teenager, he was the son of an acquaintance who owned a cabin some distance from the lodge. No choice but to call the father.

"Larry, this is Jake Morrel; it's been a long time. How are you and Betty?"

"Good, and yourself?"

"Beth and I have been right straight ahead. I don't know if you heard, but we rebuilt the old Gerard Camps."

"I did hear that. Warden Scot told me the other day that the place looks fabulous."

"Larry, I've got some bad news. I hope I'm wrong, but I think your son attempted to steal my propane supply a couple of weeks ago." After I related the story and described the truck, there was a long pause.

"It certainly sounds like your thief is my son. Let me get back to you."

After a time he called back. "I've banned my son from the family cabin for life. If you choose to press charges, I wouldn't blame you."

I decided against it, but we never made another early trip.

CHAPTER 17

◇◇◇

Hurricane Pond Gives Me a Gift

I was always on the hunt for new fishing opportunities. The Spencer Lake area was dotted with small spring-fed ponds, although not every one held wild brook trout. Some were too shallow and froze nearly to the bottom during the coldest winters, making fish survival impossible. Others had waters low in dissolved oxygen, a necessary requirement for trout. But a few had thriving populations of totally wild fish that had flourished since the ice age.

Most evenings, when I picked up the guests, a detour was planned to look for a new hotspot. When fish feed in the evening, they either suck insects from the surface or leap out of the water, grabbing the bug on the way up or down. Either method produces a circular ripple on the pond surface which expands in diameter over time. These rings stand out in the evening light. Even from one-half mile distant, a pilot can see a surface covered by intersecting rings. Not all pools holding trout were candidates for fishing locations for our guests. The water body had to be long enough for a safe take-off and landing, and aligned on an east-west axis—the direction of the prevailing wind. Over time we expanded the choices for the fishermen. Also, if a very small pond held trout, and was within walking distance of a bigger pond, we blazed a connecting trail. Usually, it was possible to land a canoe at the smaller hotspot and take off safely. (As mentioned earlier, a

Supercub can jump off the water without a rear-seat passenger.)

Hurricane Pond proved impossible to fish, since it was small, and no other water was nearby. But on scouting flights, I was intrigued by a beaver house on the south shore. Something reflective protruded from the pile of sticks. Finally, a day arrived with the perfect light, and steady wind to permit a safe takeoff and landing. The Supercub eased into Hurricane with room to spare. After taxiing over to the shore, I tied off near the animal's old house. The interlocking sticks and branches of the deserted structure were piled against an old aluminum canoe.

A couple of hard pulls separated the canoe from the rotten sticks. The craft was a very old, 14-foot Grumman. Unlike today's models, the bow and stern had compartments with waterproof round covers. A rusted 5-gallon metal potato chip can also came free. Inside was a decayed tent and sleeping bag. Not wanting to steal someone else's property, after turning the find upside down and recording the serial number, I took off.

During the next supply run to Greenville, I found flying warden Gary Dumond and told my story.

"Let me check the list of stolen boats with that serial number," he said, and did it on the spot.

"Nope, not listed," Gary reported. "I'll record the number, and you can help yourself to the canoe if it's possible to fly it out of Hurricane. But be careful, Jake," the older man advised. "Don't bust up a plane for the sake of an old canoe."

Weeks went by before an ideal day arrived to remove the prize. A steady west wind blew without gusts. Under those conditions the Supercub could take off in half the normal distance. After securing the craft to the pontoons, I taxied to the extreme east end of Hurricane and swung the plane into the wind just a couple wing lengths from shore. The old girl was off in half the pond.

The Grumman Boat Company had an exhibit at the Boxborough, Sportsman Show the next year. As a publicity stunt, the company was offering to trade a brand new craft, of the winner's choice, for the oldest aluminum canoe found in New England. The representative told me, based on the serial number, that the Hurricane canoe was a real antique. He encouraged me to enter. Later on, a letter informed me that my entry placed second.

Years later, more information came to light over cocktails with Lindley Godson, a forester for the Hollingsworth and Whitney Company. (He later rose up to become head of northeast operations of its successor, the Scott Paper Company.) Lin was a WWII ace, flying Corsairs, and hired on after the conflict ended. I had gotten to know him when I worked for Folsom's Air Service. When I related the story of the Hurricane Pond canoe, Lin thought for a moment and said, "Jake, we had operations in that part of Maine right after the war. Thinking back, I'm nearly positive that the boys who lived in the lumber camps stashed canoes in Hurricane and Douglass Ponds. I think you found one."

CHAPTER 18

◇◇◇

Fact Plus Fiction

Several weeks after returning by train from the Montreal Sportsman Show in 1980, the afternoon mail included an oversized envelope embossed with the logo of a Canadian outdoor-themed magazine. The publication was familiar, and boasted of a huge circulation. Within the envelope was a lengthy proposal, and also a contract between Hardscrabble Lodge and the magazine. The publishers wanted us to host and guide a professional hunter/writer for a week at no cost, and in return they agreed to feature a long article about the Camps in a future issue.

We thought long and hard about the pluses and minuses of the deal. Obviously, the resultant publicity was impossible to buy. However, other guests might feel slighted if we devoted too much interest to one man. Also, the odds of the writer shooting a deer were low. Then, less than 20 percent of Maine deer hunters were successful, and that number has dropped since… (Several reasons: First, the great majority of would-be hunters never *learned* to hunt. Gone are the days when grandfather took grandson under his wing to pass on his knowledge. Second, many hunters go to camp to party, not to hunt. At the time we ran Hardscrabble, the Jackman hotels hired hookers from Canada and Boston for the season. And there are less hunters in general as a diminishing percentage of today's younger generation hunts because so many prefer electronic entertainment.)

In the end we returned the paperwork with several conditions. One, we wanted to schedule the hunt at the tail end of the season. By that time the weather is cold enough and the snowpack is deep enough that few hunters choose to book reservations. Two, we stressed that the writer must be in good physical shape. Walking for hours uphill and down is strenuous activity. Three, the article must be published regardless of the hunt's outcome. The publishers agreed to our conditions and indicated that the author trained regularly and had climbed mountains in the West. Good to go!

During the summer, I received a phone call from the writer, Norman.

"Hello, Jake. I wanted to let you know that my girlfriend, Elizabeth, is going to be coming too."

"Oh...okay," I responded.

Her presence struck me as unusual, but to show good faith we welcomed her. Perhaps she, too, was a hunter. Many women hold Maine Guide licenses, and I personally have hunted with several accomplished sportswomen.

Sure enough, the last week of November was frigid, and snow covered the ground to a depth of one foot in places. The lake was partially covered with ice, so our two guests could not fly in by floatplane. Earlier, we had purchased a military-surplus tracked vehicle to utilize under these circumstances. We met Norman at the State Road, 18 miles away, and enjoyed a slow, scenic ride back in. Roaring fires burned in the lodge fireplace and in Norman's cabin when everyone arrived.

"Wow, I'm impressed," said Elizabeth.

After a wonderful meal, we retired to the armchairs and sofa in front of the fire. Norman regaled us with tales of the many sponsored hunts he had enjoyed. He had indeed traveled widely. It was soon obvious that his clothes, outerwear, footwear, guns and scopes, were donated by manufacturers, realizing that the items would appear in photographs.

Burt and I were concerned about his choice in firearms. The custom-built rifle was designed to shoot long distances accurately, and was equipped with an expensive adjustable scope. The scope had covers attached and a reticule within, used to gauge drop at hundreds of yards. Burt got the assignment to deal with the issue.

"Norm, I'm really concerned about your gun. We're going to be hunting in snowy, wet conditions where scopes are useless. We'll be lucky to see 100 feet, half the time. We'll catch a glimpse of a deer for just a few seconds. Please, take my Browning auto that my father gave me. He got it from Gramps. This baby has killed some deer."

"Burt, that's generous of you. Unfortunately, the magazine and the gunsmith would have my ass if I don't use the rifle!"

Burt and I had found several deer living on the west side of Spencer that had not been hunted hard earlier in the month. We decided to concentrate our efforts in that area, one-half to three-quarters of a mile through the woods from camp. We would slowly approach the area, spread out as far as possible, but remain in sight of each other. Burt, a master deer-sign interpreter, would use a series of hand signs to alert Norman to what was ahead.

The next morning at daylight, Burt, Norman, and I struck out, slowly west. (Elizabeth turned out to be a reader, not a hunter.) Light snow was falling, and a fresh two inches lay on the ground—perfect conditions for tracking. After no more than one hour of slow, uphill walking, we crossed the first fresh track. Burt signaled Norman that does were meandering while browsing. Within minutes, I caught a glimpse of a small doe. Norman had resolved to shoot only a large buck. By early afternoon when the time came to reverse course, we had spotted additional does, but no bucks.

The good news was the discovery of a traveling track made by a buck on a mission.

"Norm, that is a heavy deer track!" said Burt. "Two hundred pounds plus! He's trolling for does, hoping to get lucky. We've been into deer all day. He won't go far. Jake, don't you agree?"

"Norman, I've hunted with Burt for years. The man thinks like a deer. If he says it, believe it!"

The second day was almost an exact repeat of the first: no glimpse of a trophy. The second night, Beth and I sensed tension between Elizabeth and Norman. She was anxious, and he was attempting to smooth things over.

Temperature was just above zero on the third day. Burt, Norm, and I walked most of the morning, and no one saw a deer. We gathered to eat our sandwiches and candy bars in an effort to renew our energy. About an hour later, Burt spotted a large buck standing in thick growth 75 yards ahead. By placing several fingers above his head and then touching his eyes he conveyed the message.

Norman quickly saw the animal. He lowered himself on one knee, fumbled with the scope covers and adjusted the scope. Too much time, the prize had vanished. At least Norman had seen a huge deer.

After supper, Norm pulled me aside. "Jake, I've got bad news! We have to leave. Liz and I have been fighting every night. Maybe you've heard through the walls. She says if we don't travel tomorrow, we're done. I think we're done period, but that's not your worry. Please keep chasing that monster, and send me photos if you score. Jake, I feel like shit! You two have busted your asses for me, and Liz screwed the whole thing up. I wasn't thinking when she asked to go."

"Don't kick yourself. I'm sure I would have said yes, too, if she had asked me."

I was disappointed, but did not attempt to persuade him to stay. Elizabeth, red-eyed, showed for breakfast the next morning. She was polite, but virtually silent. After the meal, the military "Weasel" waded through the new snow and conveyed our guests to civilization.

We caught up with the buck late Friday afternoon. Burt killed the deer with his shotgun. We hurriedly field-dressed the animal and suspended him as high as possible. Night was already falling when we set a compass course for Hardscrabble.

"Thank goodness!" Beth said, when we walked in and stamped off our boots. "I was getting so worried; you never come home after dark."

We explained what had happened, and she was relieved.

Normally, at least six men took short turns dragging a deer. Since Burt and I were alone, we had no choice but to attempt the task by ourselves. Burt weighed nearly 300 pounds and was solid. At that time I weighed 200. Even with 500 pounds pulling 200, we were exhausted by the time we got back to the lodge and were able to take photographs of Norman's trophy.

The article appeared several months later. Included were beautiful photographs of Hardscrabble and the deer photo we had mailed to Canada. But something looked out of place in the panoramic photo of the cabins and lodge taken after sunset. Soon I realized that a full moon had been added over the lodge. Not only was the moon added, but it was placed in the north where it couldn't have existed. The copy was accurate until the time of Norman's departure. From that point on, he related the tale exactly as it happened with one exception: his name had been substituted for Burt's. Every time I read a magazine story I think of that article.

CHAPTER 19

◇◇◇

I Need You Guys to Move Three Cabins...Two Miles

Carl and I often tackled side jobs if we could mesh the chore with the demands of Hardscrabble. Usually, we were contacted because we had access to a float or ski plane which made the task much easier. One summer, Connie called in on the radio.

"Howdy, Jake. There's a man named Christopher Buckley, the third, who phoned and is very anxious to reach you.

"Connie, did he say why?"

"No, he was kind of vague, but mentioned something about a business deal."

"Could you do me a favor and call him back; tell him I'll be in Greenville on Friday and will get in touch." (We never talked business on Folsom's radio because a couple dozen remote residents regularly listened in for entertainment.)

"By the way," Connie said, "years ago, Dick flew the man's father on a regular basis. The elder Buckley's a wealthy businessman and Jake, I mean really loaded."

On the phone, Christopher was quick to the point. His family had owned a set of three old log cabins for decades. As was the usual arrangement, the cabins sat on a paper company lease. Some time ago, he had inherited the cabins and had used them sporadically. The land had recently been swapped to another large landholder who had evicted all the lease holders because the forest was now designated as a Conservation Area. The original lessor, as a gesture of goodwill, had granted the Buckley heirs a new location two miles down the shoreline.

Finally, he asked, "Can you and Carl move my camps over the ice to the new land within one year?"

"Well, to be honest, the answer to your question is a BIG maybe. Given ideal conditions, which include thick ice with little snow cover, the move would be labor-intensive, but possible. The problem is that those conditions don't occur every winter. We also would have to find and fell a dozen good-sized trees in order to fabricate skids. The skids need to be placed in the fall. So if the winter does not cooperate, you're out of luck, and your money will be down the drain. You are going to be taking a huge gamble. Why don't I fly in tomorrow, check everything out and get back to you?" I replied.

"Don't worry about me losing money. I can afford to piss away the cash," Buckley said.

Saturday's flight to that northern lake gave me hope. Both sites were adjacent to the water, and the cabins were sound, having been maintained by the father. Also, numerous 15-inch-diameter straight pines grew around the buildings. We would have ample material to construct skids.

After estimating the time and risk of the project, Carl and I submitted a padded bid, with the reservation that if the ice was not fit during the winter, we would keep half of the fee paid in advance. Without hassle, the bid was accepted. Within days, a bank check was in the mail. We were working for a customer we had never met.

In early October, we flew in to jack the camps and construct skids. The buildings, tinder dry from age, lifted easily using high-lift jacks. Logs were cut and notched to make two lengthwise heavy skids, interconnected by cross pieces. Cables, tightened diagonally by heavy "come-alongs," stabilized the structures. By late afternoon of the second day, three skids were cut, and one cabin sat two feet in the air on a finished skid. Time for cocktail hour.

As we sipped bourbon, a floatplane cleared the ridge, made a lazy circle, and touched down near the site. Out stepped a man, who had to be Christopher, carrying a Maine pack basket. Max, the pilot, flew home to supper.

Mr. Buckley was nervous.

"Want a drink?" I asked.

"No thanks, I'll just take a look around."

After walking around the structure, he said, "Nice job, men."

"We're going to cook some dinner. Care to join?" I said, heading to one of the buildings.

"I brought my own, but thanks," he said. He set a box of saltines and two cans of sardines on the table. Next he produced a newish revolver and laid the gun next to his food.

Carl and I said nothing at first. Later, I asked, "What's the firearm for?"

"I'm certainly not staying in the woods overnight unarmed," he said.

Okay!

Before anyone took a bite of food, our friend asked, "Is it possible to call Greenville?"

I produced a portable Folsom's radio.

Chris said, "Tell Max to turn around and pick me up."

"Yo, Max, Jako here, do you copy?"

"Jako, what the hell do you want now? I'm just pulling in."

"Mr. Buckley has decided to leave."

"Goddamn him! Just like his old man; crazy as a shit-house rat! Tell him it's gonna cost him overtime!"

"He says fine."

Thirty minutes later, Mr. Buckley departed and never came in again!

During the next two days, we set the other two buildings on logs, then flew home to wait for March.

Terry, a logger from Brownville, who owned a large log skidder fitted with a powerful winch, agreed to haul the buildings across Jo Mary. Mother Nature was on our side the first week of March. Several feet of ice covered the lake and the surface held almost no snow. Carl and I flew in on skis the day before our appointment. Terry wanted to start at daylight in order to drive the several miles, through two feet of snow, from a logging road to the shore.

"It's eight o'clock, where is he?" I said to Carl.

I took off in the plane to have a look. Fresh skidder tracks covered the landscape. Back and forth, back and forth they went. I spotted a black plume of diesel smoke not far away. Terry looked up and acknowledged the Supercub. In repeated passes I buzzed him toward the cabins, and he caught on. Soon the machine sat next to the buildings.

The rest was anticlimactic. Terry winched the front of the first skid into the air and moved forward. The skid slid along on the ice—so easily, he could keep shifting to higher gears. At the far shore he spun the building around and used the winch to pull it well inland. The next two moved just as easily. Because of deep snow drifts, it was impossible to determine whether rocks rested below, but that was beyond the scope of our agreement. All three buildings were on the new lease and the job was done. Terry had a straight track to follow home. We flew to Greenville.

Following an exchange of photographs, we got another check. Christopher never contacted me again.

CHAPTER 20

◇◇◇

Insect Invasions

Three times they arrived out of the blue: millions of insects surrounded the lodge. Each invasion affected the operation of Hardscrabble in a different way, because three different species were involved. Each swarm was a once-in-a-lifetime experience.

Spruce-budworm events occur at about 40-year intervals. This cycle has been documented since the early settlements in Maine. The caterpillars suddenly multiply rapidly and proceed to eat the fresh growth of fir trees, eventually killing the softwood forest. Until the modern era, the insect advanced like an army through the woods, constantly searching for new food. Soon the horde exhausted the available supply, and the population collapsed. Modern technology has allowed aerial spraying of the dying trees in an effort to delay mortality. A dying tree has commercial value, a dead forest does not. The result of spraying, however, was a budworm infestation that lasted for years, because new food did not run out.

Maybe it's because they flew every day on the precipice of a disaster, but spray-pilots were often characters, and dozens gathered in the small towns with airstrips selected for operations centers. (Aerial application is one of the most dangerous of all jobs.) Many were middle-aged WWII pilots, faces crisscrossed with sun-burned wrinkles and squint lines. Most smoked steadily, and found the bars in the evenings. But those boys could fly an airplane. Several times, returning to the Jackman Airport after a mission, they rolled the wheels of the ex-military TBMs along the surface of Big Wood Lake, sending up a rooster tail of water. The TBMs were selected by the State Forest Service because the terrain surrounding both Jackman and nearby Hardscrabble was mountainous. The huge spray tankers used in the flat country to the north were useless. The skilled pilots would start at the top of a mountain valley and spray downslope, hugging the treetops all the way to the bottom.

Weeks before the spraying commenced, people with private or commercial camps located in the application area were summoned to a meeting where temporary restrictions were explained.

The project leader from the Maine Forest Service, Cecil, addressed the gathering.

"We plan to spray for the next three weeks. Usually, flights will be planned for early morning and late afternoon. The wind has to be almost calm to minimize spray drift. Since we don't know which days will permit operations, to protect the public we'll be chaining all woods-roads for the duration. I know this policy will create hardships for everyone. Understand, we have no choice. We can't just let the valuable forest die.

"Now, take a close look at the preliminary spray map, and let me know if you see problem areas around your leases."

"Cecil, this sucks! Not everyone can fly like Jake. How do you expect us to get out for supplies?"

"Essentially, most of you will be out of luck for the whole time. If we expect several days of rain or high winds, we will open the gate for a while. But all of your leases clearly state that the lessor retains the right to close the road at their discretion."

"How will we know if the road is open?"

"We've got no way to let you know. But if it's pouring, the gate chain should be down. Folks, I'm sorry about this."

I carefully examined the spray map of the area around our

lease, looking for complications.

"Cecil, this stream valley running from the camps up toward Little Enchanted contains our gravity-water system. We can't do without water!" The official crosshatched the map along the pipe so the final version could be amended.

Beth and I expected that guests would be irritated by the 4:30 am flights of the pilots, and we apologized in advance. Such was not the case! At the first sound of the huge radial engines, the entire group was out on the lawn watching the air show. Repeatedly, the TBMs dove down toward Spencer Lake discharging the loads. The noise was deafening, since three or four planes worked together. One morning we watched a pilot approaching a small ridge, about to begin the plunge. Misjudging the height of the crest, and coming in a tad low, he discharged the entire load. Branches shattered like match sticks.

And then it happened! The deafening roar of 1700 horsepower dove right at our small crowd. The old fighter plane was 50 feet above the treetops, twisting its way down the course of the stream behind the main lodge, the source of our drinking water!

"What the x$#&! This area was marked out-of-bounds!" I was wild, jumped in the Supercub, and flew to Jackman.

"That's our only water source! I told you about this…"

"Jake—"

"You marked it down…

"I know, Jake—"

"What kind of incompetence lets this happen! I can't believe…"

I was spitting words instead of talking.

Finally, he held up both hands. "Jake, I don't doubt your word. Take these water-specimen bottles, sample the brook, and fly them back in. We can test for spray. If your stream has been contaminated, we'll supply gallons of drinking water until it clears. I'm truly sorry. Sometimes these cowboys make mistakes."

The stream tested positive, and I flew in a lot of free State water.

During another spring, we were at peak season. Fly-fishing was excellent, and as a result, the lodge was full. Gradually, during morning and evening flights, I noticed that the small, pale green hardwood leaves were vanishing. At 50 feet above the treetops, the devastation was obvious. Also, on my escape walks out the access road, it was hard to miss the green caterpillars constantly crossing the gravel. After a rain, some of the puddles harbored small rafts of the critters, literally paddling across the water. Day by day, the trees took on the look of winter.

Then one day, hundreds of caterpillars, locked together in a three-foot square raft, were slowly drifting with the wind across Spencer Lake. The same rafts appeared in the small trout ponds, sometimes several at once. The fish seemed uninterested in the protein, but the appearance hurt the image of a pristine mountain pond, and the trees without leaves in the spring looked odd.

The last episode, the next year, was crippling to lodge operations. Beth always hung the white camp sheets out to dry on a long double clothesline. The strong sun, combined with the wind, gave the bedding a fresh smell. She started to notice what appeared to be large houseflies clinging to the fabric. But the insects were not common houseflies. A fast hand is necessary to capture one of those; these new residents would crawl all over your arm.

They multiplied day by day. Whole sheets were densely covered. The ropes securing the plane and boats doubled in diameter. Boat seats and cushions were black. My wife was a sun-worshipper, and tried to lie out for an hour a day between chores. I had to construct a large, screen-wire box to shelter her. Even so, little sun penetrated. As guests walked around the camp yard, flies covered their bodies.

One by one, the sports departed. We stopped taking new reservations. The loss of income was a major setback.

Numerous rumors circulated about the infestation. Some claimed that the lethargic creatures always followed the caterpillars by one year. Others said that the Canadians had released the pests as predators for the remaining defoliators. We never knew for sure. That year was a hard lesson about unforeseen circumstances ruining your fortune.

CHAPTER 21

◇◇◇

Midnight Train to Montreal

At one time, the Canadian Pacific Railroad Company ran a luxurious passenger train from coast to coast across Canada. When the train line was constructed before 1900, the company selected the most direct route possible across the continent, given the terrain. For this reason, tracks cross the State of Maine from Vanceboro in the east to Lowelltown in the west, passing through Greenville along the way. This quirk of design made it possible for Beth and me to travel easily from Greenville to Montreal (farther west), although we had to depart when the engine pulled into our stop, just after midnight.

We were always looking for new ways to reach potential customers for Hardscrabble, so one year we decided to place a display booth in the Montreal Sportsman Show, which took place over a long weekend. Good friends agreed to travel with us, allowing for an opportunity to mix pleasure and business.

Transporting a display, which included a full-mounted large buck, required some innovation. I devised a crate on wheels with a plastic cage to protect the taxidermy. Two people could lift the box, in order to heft it on to the elevated baggage-car floor.

On a cold winter night, we waited for the brilliant train headlight to approach from the east. Right on schedule, the locomotive stopped at the small station. The crew members were very helpful and amused by our baggage.

Montreal was a vibrant city. Excellent restaurants were abundant, the streets were totally safe, even at night, and boutique shops were scattered about. Unlike Greenville, almost everyone on the street was stylishly dressed. Christmas spirit permeated the air. We met many potential guests and enjoyed fine meals after the show closed in the evenings.

The return trip was scheduled for Monday night, so we decided to check our cargo during the early afternoon. Wise choice!

The baggage handler took one look at the deer and said, "Folks, we've got a problem here. Canadian regulations prohibit the transportation of any animal, living or dead, without a vets tag."

"Whoa, hold on here," I said. "That deer came into Canada on a CP train and no one said boo! It's worth more than a thousand dollars, so we certainly can't leave him behind."

"Sir, I'm sorry if some other employee screwed up, but I'm not about to lose my job because of your deer!"

"Where is your supervisor?" I asked.

"See that little office ahead to the right? Go right ahead and bend his ear!"

I was naive. A twenty-dollar bill would have resolved our dilemma.

We proceeded to speak with supervisor after supervisor of increasingly higher rank. All seconded their underling. What to do? One of our companions was a lawyer, and he suggested a call to The United States Consulate. After a lengthy conversation, the officer in charge said that he would contact CP Rail corporate headquarters and discuss the matter. He suggested we check back in two hours.

The second phone call brought the news that a solution had been negotiated, and we were to report to the corporate office at four o'clock.

Our cab pulled up to an impressive building; massive stonework soared, story after story. Inside, we were escorted through deep-pile carpeted halls whose walls were hung with large oil paintings and portraits. Everyone wore blue or black three-piece suits, and not a hair was misplaced. We were offered heavy leather chairs in a large conference room, the location of a unique signing ceremony.

"An exception will be made in order for you to return home," said the vice president in charge. "However, you have to agree never to bring the crate back to Canada."

Seven or eight pages of verbiage were required to state those facts. Beth and I had to initial every page and sign the last one. The vice president signed with a signature several times the size of ours.

Back to the train station.

I was uncomfortable with the prospect of confronting the baggage handler who had initially refused the cargo. It became apparent that he had been briefed.

With a wide smile on his face, he said, "Load the crate onto this cart toward the front."

He made no effort to help! By lifting one end at a time, I heaved it on.

"Now get on and sit behind the box."

"Wait just a second," I said. "I'm not getting on that wagon."

"Sir, it says in the agreement that you will accompany the animal. It means just that!"

"Nothing was said about this downtown!" I stated.

"Maybe they just forgot. You can go back and talk to them. Remember, the train leaves in an hour!"

He had me, so I sat like a fool on the cart.

"Now make sure you keep your arms and legs in front of you. The chute is narrow."

The smiling attendant pushed the cart up to a tunnel-like entryway, with an opening just slightly larger than the width of the crate. Beth had a concerned look on her face.

I quipped, "Don't worry, the baggage survives this every day."

To say the least, though, I was anxious and pissed off.

"Whoosh!" He pushed the baggage trolley into...darkness!

The gradual ramp downstairs was basically a hardwood passage which forced the cart through a 180-degree turn before reaching the platform. I bounced off the left and right surface repeatedly on the way down. It was a damned good thing my arms were in front!

Another employee loaded the deer into a baggage car and was nice enough to find a couple of shipping quilts to serve as my seat on the floor. After a while, the train jerked, and we were on the way to Greenville. There was one light in the car, and I saw that no other freight was aboard. After maybe 15 minutes, an older conductor appeared to collect my ticket. After seeing me sitting on the mats, he said, "Come with me, Son."

We ended up in the caboose. I was amazed to discover that the last car on the train was outfitted like a motel room. Armchairs, plush carpets, a refrigerator, and a large selection of snacks were in place.

"Make yourself at home. Want a scotch?"

Ha! After that one, I was offered another. What a transformation of fortune. That turned out to be the most pleasant train ride of my life!

N24446, a 1941 Taylorcraft, was the plane Jake flew to build time and experience.

Jake used parts from three damaged Edo 1320 floats to build this new set.

Beth surveying the remains of the old camps for the first time.

Hardscrabble was nestled between steep ridges next to this protected narrows.

Our daughter Thea sitting in front of the new Hardscrabble fireplace.

Carl and Jake stayed in this cabin during the first winter of reconstruction.

Cabin number six, freshly reconstructed.

Hardscrabble's Supercub, with repaired right wing, tied down during the first winter.

Jake, driving the "Bomby" doubletrack, ferrying a load of supplies.

Beth, hard at work in the log kitchen.

The guests enjoyed Beth's popovers!

A hearty meal with draft beer was always appreciated by the men.

The Hardscrabble hunting tent, complete with wood stove.

Jake preparing to fly a large deer out of Roaring Brook Pond.

Keith standing next to the large deer he chased for most of the week.

Millions of these huge flies invaded Spencer Lake one summer.

This painting of Spencer Lake was a gift from a talented guest.

Jake and Carl flew this Aeronca Sedan from Virginia back to Hardscrabble.

Our son Zeke never lacked for entertainment at Hardscrabble.

Beth and I are enjoying retirement at ME32, our home and airstrip.

CHAPTER 22

◇◇◇

Eight Very Long Miles

During the winter, Hardscrabble was only open for guests on weekends. Most customers were ice fishermen who arrived on their own snowmobiles. The men cooked their own meals on propane stoves installed in each camp. Beth, Thea, and Zeke usually remained at our home in Greenville, while I traveled to camp. The summer conveniences of running water and inside plumbing were not available. Instead, we provided two outhouses and kept an ice hole for drinking water. After water was dipped, the hole was covered over with insulating fir boughs. Most guests expected Spartan accommodations in the winter, and were happy just to have a warm cabin next to the lake.

I always hoped for decent flying weather on Thursdays (travel day). (The return schedule was more flexible. Given a warm camp, plenty of food, and radio communication to Greenville, a delay of a couple days because of weather was merely an inconvenience.) Winter weather, though, is often miserable. Storms and high winds are common. When that was the case, flying was abandoned, and the ride to Spencer Lake was time-consuming.

We owned a 1966 Skidoo Alpine double-track snowmobile. Double-tracks were designed by Bombardier as working sleds, able to haul heavy loads. We also owned a 10-foot-long "moose" sled, which coupled to the machine. The "Bomby" could easily move hundreds of pounds of freight. On a few occasions, I hauled four men seated on cushions placed on the wooden bed. The machine had previously been ridden by an elderly Greenville man, and had been perfectly maintained. I installed a more modern Rotex 399 engine and a Comet clutch, and replaced the track bearings. After the rebuild, the machine purred along at 15 to 20 miles an hour effortlessly.

Given bad weather, my trip to Hardscrabble began in Greenville, the snowmobile having been loaded aboard our pickup. Driving time to Parlin Pond was about an hour. After unloading the Alpine, another hour-long snowmobile ride lay ahead.

On one return trip, for the first ten miles, the Skidoo hummed along as usual. Then, at the bottom of Bear Hill, the engine pitch changed. Funny—being a mechanic, I always expected a breakdown because I knew how complicated any engine was. But that had never happened before.

Said I to myself: *Shit, it's either a spark plug or a head gasket. Hope it's a plug, that's easy. Get real, Jake, plugs don't foul at cruising power, and the engine is hissing. Old buddy, you've blown a head gasket.*

The machine still ran, but only at partial power.

Okay, if I can get it to climb this two-mile hill, it's flat to the highway.

Halfway to the top it came to a halt.

Damn! I have to try again.

I jumped off, grabbed the rear end, and slid it on the snow to face the reverse direction. The Alpine sailed down the grade and beyond, so a run at the hill was possible. Off the machine, yank it around! Full throttle toward the hill. The second attempt beat the first, but not by much. I was stranded six miles from a road before the invention of the cell phone.

All the variables raced through my brain. *Supposed to warm up tonight and rain late. Monday's going to bring heavy rain followed by high winds and plunging temperatures. I can't stay the night and hike out tomorrow. This sucks! If I wait until tomorrow morning to walk out that means attempting to fix Bomby in the brutal cold. That's out of the question! Get your ass in gear. If I start now and hoof it, I can be at Julie and Andy's camp a few hours after dark. I'll surprise them!*

Unfortunately, heavy felt-lined packs, designed for warmth, not walking, weighed down my size-14 feet. Your feet slide fore and aft in a pack with each step. Soon, due to the friction, my soles were on fire. Nothing to do but take large strides and persevere.

Darkness arrived, but an all-white landscape and some moonlight made night vision possible. Every time a chorus of coyote howls resonated through the valley, my woodsman's common sense had to reassure my natural reaction of fear. *Jake, remember—it's a fact: every animal in the Maine woods is afraid of and will avoid humans.* Talking to myself just barely kept panic at bay while intensely strong canines with powerful jaws were so close!

After *four hours* I reached the road, and thirty minutes (and two miles) after that, I was sitting in a cozy cabin. My good friends, who lived on Parlin Pond, treated me to a warm meal, offered their phone, prepared my bed, and volunteered their snow machine for the rescue effort. After supper, the bourbon soothed my throbbing feet.

The plan was for Beth to leave Greenville as early as possible the next morning. First, she would gather tools, rain suits, and a tarp, buy a replacement gasket plus spare, and make arrangements for Thea and Zeke to stay with friends. According to the forecast, rain would start before she left.

My wife arrived in our truck, in a deluge with the necessary supplies. The heavy rain had transformed the trail into a sheet of ice, covered with water. Neither machine was fitted with track studs. That meant the slightest burst of the throttle sent the rescue sled into a spin. To top it off, Beth hated snowmobiles and did everything in her power to avoid them. Since she would have to drive out on one of the snowmobiles alone, she drove in for practice. After much excitement, including several 360s and 180s, the crippled Alpine lay ahead.

We cut poles from nearby exposed alders and fashioned a tent over the Skidoo with the tarp. The repair was easy, and two hours later, a full-strength beast was ready to go. Beth went ahead slowly and I followed. We soon were back with our friends enjoying a welcome cocktail hour.

CHAPTER 23

◇◇◇

The Men Who Missed Dinner

Hundreds of men flew out of Hardscrabble Lodge to more remote locations in the morning and returned before nightfall, able to enjoy supper in comfort. Six men missed the evening meal. What follows are their stories. Names have been changed because several spent a frigid night outside stalked by fear that no one would choose to remember.

One of the trips the more adventurous fishermen enjoyed was a daylong paddle from the dam on Spencer Lake, down Little Spencer Stream, then continuing on Big Spencer Stream to the dead-water area below Flagstaff Lake. In order to make the trip possible, I flew the fishermen and a canoe to the dam, and picked up on the dead-water in the evening. This approach made it possible for sports to enjoy a leisurely float and to access completely remote parts of the flowage. However, we gave explicit instructions to each fisherman who opted for the potentially dangerous trip.

"Be on the lookout for the one huge, solitary pine tree, growing on a long, narrow island in Big Spencer Stream. At that point, make a slight right turn; it leads to the start of the long flat-water location where we'll pick you up in the evening. Listen up: if you turn left instead of right, very shortly you're going to be confronted by the Dead River Gorge. You'll probably hear the ten-foot waterfall, feeding a raging torrent. This is considered to be some of the roughest water in Maine."

About the time I was fueling the Supercub for the evening trip, our guests, Hal and Burt, were unfortunately bearing left and approaching the falls. Furiously, they back-paddled. It was much too late and to no avail. The canoe crashed into the foam and was swept along by four- and five-foot waves downstream.

Flying 500 feet above the ground, the pilot has a panoramic vantage point. Within a couple of miles of the dead-water I saw that no canoe was in sight. Suspecting a couple of over-eager anglers, I continued to fly the stream network, top to bottom, in an effort to locate them. Hal and Burt, and my canoe, had simply vanished.

They must be down the Dead River? No. Initially, my brain did not accept that possibility. Excuses came first. *Maybe they're just hidden and I can't see them—beneath some trees, on the shore. Maybe the canoe got swamped and sank in the flat water?* But quickly, my common sense overcame emotion. The reality was that chances were as good as not that both were injured or worse.

Crap, it's getting dark and I need fuel. I'll fly down the gorge for a couple miles. There's an outside chance a clue will materialize.

It did. First I saw a submerged cooler, then a life jacket, and finally, a badly twisted 18-foot canoe. Not good! After a short ways, I reversed my direction and headed upstream, flying the plane as slowly as possible. And then the impossible! Two soaked men were sitting on a boulder above the stream, below the steep side walls of the small canyon. Circling several times, I made sure they realized that help was coming.

I flew back to camp and ran to the lodge.

"Beth, the men missed the turn on Spencer and crashed over the falls. God damn it, I can't believe it. The good news is that I saw them both downstream and they were soaked, but moving. No way to know about injuries, but both were sitting and waving. The canoe is history. I've got to reach Folsom's if anyone is still in the office.

"Max, Connie, Dick—anyone—pick up! It's Jake, and I've got guests in big trouble."

"Jake, it's Dick. I'm over at the house, and Connie and the pilots have gone home. What's going on?"

"Dick, two of our men crashed their canoe over Grand Falls into the Dead. I could see them from the air one-half mile below Spencer Stream. They were seated, and waved to me. Call the Fish and Game and notify a warden. I'll stand by." I waited for him to make the call.

"Jake, I reached the dispatcher. A warden is headed toward the river. Good Luck! Let me know what happens. I'll be up 'til ten. Call if you need anything."

Given the exact location of the men, the warden patrolling the Dead River region figured out how to use old four-wheel drive roads to travel within walking distance of Hal and Burt. Several hours later, both men, shaken but not seriously injured, were on the way to the dam-keeper's cabin on Flagstaff Lake. Once there, they were treated to a large meal, prepared by the dam-keeper's wife at midnight. The next morning she prepared a sumptuous breakfast, which I also enjoyed, having flown over to retrieve both men.

Hal was a talented artist. The following winter, Beth and I received a package, which turned out to be a beautiful painting of the view looking down Spencer Lake from Hardscrabble. I was relieved that the serenity of his time with us made as much of an impact as his wipe-out. That reminder hangs in my home today.

Another pair who got into trouble were Luke and Pete, who had flown into Hardscrabble three different years, right at the peak of fishing season. A father-and-son team, each was competent, competitive, and dedicated. If it rained, the only boat that fished until dark was theirs. Each time we flew to a remote pond, Luke gently reminded me to pick them up last. The point was made, and I always complied. I guess I just admired their drive and enthusiasm. Fishermen who consistently do well certainly don't hurt your reputation.

Father and son shared one major goal on the third visit. That wish was to visit Blakesly Pond, the smallest we fished, but usually the best. Mother Nature had conspired against the men for two seasons in a row. The reason many sports never got a chance to enjoy the thrill had to do with prevailing wind direction and the size of the lake. The Supercub could easily *land* in its length with a safety margin—given a wind from the north. However, even a north wind would not permit a safe *takeoff* with the added weight of a passenger. Everyone had to come out on foot. In order to get picked up in the evening, a Blakesly angler had to walk down a marked trail to a logging road and then walk about two miles to Baker Pond. Average time for a middle-aged man was, give or take, one and one-half hours. When we approached Blakesly in the morning, I made a habit of flying parallel to the evening route, to orient the men to the pickup trek.

The perfect conditions materialized mid-week for Luke and Peter. By eight o'clock they were casting away.

As darkness approached that evening, I flew the four or five miles to Baker Lake. No one was there. I sat in the plane until the far shore dimmed. Immediately after takeoff, the opening of the trail came into view, but details on the ground were invisible. Then after a mile or so, I saw two bobbing flashlights. The darkness was much too total to return, but at least both men were safe.

In early summer, long before the sun rises, a dim light appears throughout the sky. Once your eyes adjust, a pilot can see to fly before four o'clock on a clear morning. I landed on Baker Pond about that time and encountered two fishermen, thrilled to see me.

Over breakfast the whole story of the previous night was related between bites of Beth's homemade French toast.

"Dad, what the hell made us think we could sprint out of there in 45 minutes? You talk about stupid!"

"Pete, I take full responsibility. I should have put my foot down and demanded that we leave; dumb, dumb, dumb! Twice your age and I acted like a kid! It's no excuse, but my judgment was compromised by the fishing. Jake, you won't believe this, but large trout jumped everywhere. If Hardscrabble didn't have a catch-and-release rule, we could have easily kept our limit of big fish. So, an extra five minutes led to ten and then fifteen, and well, you know the rest.

"Jake, what walks around the shore and splashes in and out of the water in the dark?" Luke asked.

"That had to be a moose," I said.

"Dad, how close do you think those howling coyotes were? I swear they sounded close enough to see in the day."

"Pete, I don't know, but I'll agree—they were close, and I'm some glad they didn't come any closer. I don't mind telling you now, I was scared shitless! All the weird noises were the worst of it. I had no idea how many animals roamed at night. Jake, we heard a girl wailing and screaming before daylight. I swear—both of us heard it."

"Only two animals make that unmistakable shriek," I said. "Take your choice: bobcat or bear. A bear sounds more like a suffering woman."

"Horrible sound, went right through you. And Jake, I thought insects stopped biting at dark. They tore us up all night!"

"Actually, some species are worse after sunset. Mosquitoes and 'no-see-ums' are bad news until morning," I said.

"You know, son, that was the first time in my life I was scared for hours at a time. I'll never forget feeling so helpless. I always told you that adversity makes you stronger, and maybe we are now, but one thing is certain. You and I will never make such a stupid decision again!

"Jake, I want to apologize for my mistakes. I caused you not only to fly after dark last night, but to get up before four o'clock this morning to make an extra trip. What can I do to make it right?"

"Luke, don't give it a second thought. First, I get up at four every morning. Also, remember, if it rains for two days I don't make any flights. It all averages out in the end. You obviously learned a hard lesson, but remember the positive. You guys had the type of fishing that others dream about!"

The final two men who lost out on dinner did so on two separate occasions but under similar circumstances. During the early eighties, most of Maine was open for deer hunting in November. However, the Fish and Game Department had closed parts of the western mountains for the first week of the month due to declining deer populations resulting from several harsh winters and predation. Hardscrabble fell into the restricted area.

Since we could not afford to lose twenty-five percent of our hunting revenue, an alternative plan was hatched. We located a remote pond in an open zone and set up a tent camp large enough to house eight hunters. Burt suggested Roaring Brook Pond, near Sebec Lake. We flew two large tents, a woodstove, and cooking supplies into the pond. When finished, one tent had a long plank table, a propane range, the woodstove, and a dozen short pieces of log for seats. We even set up a beer tap supported by the tent post. The second tent provided shelter for eight men to sleep on their own air mattresses inside sleeping bags.

The challenge of hunting out of the Roaring Brook camp was navigation. Hunters stepped out of the tent in the early morning surrounded by forest without any roads for reference. Some skill and confidence with the use of a compass was essential. Burt, Carl, and I normally hunted alongside the sports to make sure no one got lost.

This particular year, two parties of four made week-long reservations. Beth and I had met one of the groups of hunters at the Harrisburg Sportsman Show. All had retired from manufacturing jobs located in the York, Pennsylvania area. During our conversation, I explained the challenge of hunting in unbroken forest. The group did not see that as a problem, but preferred a spot relatively close to camp to sit. I assured them that either Burt or I would help pick out good vantage points for still hunting, within a ten-minute walk of the tents. The other group had made reservations by phone, and I knew little about them, other than that they lived in New Jersey.

A few hours after arriving with Folsom's, one of the New Jersey men, Vincent, asked me for a private word.

"Jake, please don't take offense, but we prefer to hunt alone. We've hunted together for years, and frankly, we think you would just get in the way."

"Vincent, have any of you hunted in a roadless area like this before?" I asked.

"Three of us were in Vietnam. Does that answer your question?"

I did not force the issue, but was uncomfortable with the situation.

As the week neared its end, spirits in camp were high. Several deer and a bear had been harvested. Unfortunately, the New Jersey party had not been as lucky. Saturday dawned with a mixture of snow and rain, but everyone headed out, since it was the final day. We always advised the men to be within a short walking distance of the camp by 2:30 in the afternoon, since on overcast days in November the light fades early and rapidly. Everyone was enjoying beers by 3:30 except one of the four from New Jersey.

"Burt, I've got a shitty feeling about this. I'll bet that Vincent is going to push until it's dark. He hates the fact that they all struck out."

"Jake, you're right!"

"What sucks is that we have no clue where he is. Unless he answers a gunshot we're royally screwed! Or he is..."

Beginning at four, we fired solitary pistol shots and listened for a return. None came. With no clue where the man had ventured and no response from shots, it was pointless to commence a search. Better to wait until first light. If Vincent had made it through a tour in 'Nam, he certainly had survival skills.

As soon as I could make out the far shore of the pond, the Supercub was off. Flying expanding circles around the pond, no fluorescent hat or smoke was visible. I radioed Folsom's, explained the situation, and asked Max, the pilot, to make a couple of circles when he arrived for the pickup.

During the second orbit, Max keyed the radio mike.

"Jake, I've got him. He's walking along Roaring Brook Stream about a thousand feet below the outlet. He's not wearing a coat."

The first rule of thumb if lost as darkness descends is to stay put. Build a fire if able and attempt to stay warm. Exercise all night if necessary. Our guest did not follow those tips. He kept moving, colliding with small branches, and tripping from time to time. Encountering a brook, he followed it downstream before reversing course sometime in the night. At times he walked in the water. By morning he was without his rifle and his coat. But he was alive. I related the news to the group.

"Carl, do you want to remain in camp to help the other men board the planes? Burt and I will grab a coat and get him."

"Sure," said Carl.

We pocketed a handful of candy bars and struck out for the sport's location, more than half a mile away.

"He might be pretty weak," I said.

"Yeah...between the two of us we can carry him, if we have to," said Burt.

He spotted Vincent first, sitting on a log. As we drew closer, the pain on his face was obvious. Numerous scratches had bled, and he was soaked and filthy.

"Vincent, are you hurt?" I yelled when we were 50 feet away.

He pivoted and looked right through me.

"Here, want a candy bar?" Burt offered.

He reached for it, but when it made contact with his hand, he couldn't grasp it, and it fell to the ground. His body was not functioning well. Burt picked it up, and after removing the wrapper, held the bar to his mouth. He took a bite and then another, but did not say a word.

Finally, Vincent rose, made eye contact with me, and mumbled, "I don't want to hear a word from either one of you. Let's go."

We walked slowly and silently back to the tents. Max flew the hunter to Greenville and attempted to drive him to the local hospital, but Vincent refused. Instead, he sat in Max's bathtub while Folsom's made the additional trips to Roaring Brook. A bullet dodged!

Another lost-hunter episode happened during the second season at Roaring Brook. At 3:30, one of the older, more cautious hunters was missing. Others in his group had seen the man as late as 2:30, so he had to be close by. At 4 o'clock, just like the year before, I fired the pistol. No reply to the first or second shot. A minute later, after the third shot, a weak gunshot report came from the east. Two more shots were answered from the same direction.

I gathered together a Coleman gas lantern, two compasses, and three flashlights. Striking a course toward the east, I purposely walked slowly. By flashlight, the woods appear differently than they do in the daytime. Small branches are often invisible, and irregularities in the ground do not stand out. The only way to walk a straight-line compass course is to constantly select an object ahead that lines up on course and walk directly toward it. Since the lost hunter and I would have to find a small pond in the dark during the return trip, it was essential to be accurate. Periodically, I touched off an additional shot and always got an answer. Slowly, his gun reports changed from muted, to sharp, and then to a crack. All of a sudden we were standing face to face.

"Jake, I can't tell you how glad I am to see you. I did the dumbest thing. Just like the other days, I followed the compass back to camp, but I guess south on the case was aligned with the north needle. Somehow I walked exactly in the opposite direction."

"Don't kick yourself. Sure you screwed up, but after that you did exactly the right thing. You stayed put and I see you have a fire all set to light."

"Jake, hate to admit it, but I made another mistake. I packed my waterproof matches case, but it was empty. I used the matches during our annual Fourth of July picnic."

Returning was uneventful, and soon Harry was accepting the good-natured ribbing of the other hunters.

Pretty good stats to only lose six men!

CHAPTER 24

◇◇◇

Oops, the Bug is in My Eye!

Running a lodge did have fringe benefits. One aspect of the business that Beth and I enjoyed was downtime during the off-season. By midsummer, the water temperature of the ponds we frequented had increased to the point that dry fly-fishing suffered. We encouraged as many guests as possible to avoid those couple of weeks. After all, an angler who catches few fish is usually not a repeat customer. Occasionally, while we had the place to ourselves, a promising evening would come along with calm winds and dropping temperatures. After eating dinner, Beth and I often jumped into the Supercub and went fishing.

On one such occasion we headed for Little Enchanted Pond. That night the water surface was covered with dozens of beautiful, spreading fish-feeding circles. We were in for a thrill. Within five minutes we sat in the canoe surrounded by wild brook trout.

At the Boxborough Sportsman Show, a high-school student had approached me with a proposal. He produced a small metal box of dry flies, which he had hand-tied. His work was excellent. He asked if I would trade each dollar of the cost of his stay at Hardscrabble for one fly. He added that he did not have a driver's license, so his dad would have to come along. I so admired his spunk that I agreed. Beth and I inherited almost one thousand small dry flies. Some were red and white irritators, called "devil bugs."

Beth did the fishing that evening, and I maneuvered the canoe. We enjoyed probably the best catch of the summer. Casting while sitting in a boat requires skill. The rod is much closer to the water than in the standing position, so precise timing becomes more important. The caster's arm tires quickly, and after a while, that was the case with Beth.

"A couple more and I'm done," she said.

Almost immediately after that, she blurted, "Dammit, the bug is in my eye!"

Sure enough, Beth's eyelid was hooked by a number 22 devil bug. Using my jackknife, I cut the line next to the fly, paddled back to the Supercub, and flew back to the lodge.

Dr. Fichtner was our semi-retired country physician. He had purchased Penobscot Lodge, a remote, former-corporate retreat, as a retirement project. Doc was known for his wit, wisdom, and kindness, so I gave him a call. (The sporting camps north of Greenville shared a two-way radio network owned by Folsom's Air Service. Hence, the camp operators could talk to each other, as well as to the flying service.) Several times previously, he had gladly offered advice concerning guests' minor medical emergencies. Of course, I realized that a couple of dozen radio subscribers were listening to the conversation.

After I described our predicament, Doc asked a few questions.

"Is Beth in great pain?"

"No."

"Does the hook seem to have penetrated the eyeball?"

"No, the lid flutters and exposes the eyeball."

"Is Beth calm?"

"Yes."

"Jake, get Beth three fingers of scotch, and call me back in thirty minutes."

Time stood still during that wait.

After thirty minutes, I called back.

"Jake, slowly move your index finger toward Beth's eyeball and gently touch the lid."

"Done, Doc."

"Jake, did she flinch?"

"No, Doc, she didn't move a muscle."

"Okay Jacob, remove the fly just as I have taught you before."

That method causes the hook to come out exactly the opposite of the way that it entered. I placed my finger on the top of the fly shank where the fishing line had been secured. Then I looped a short piece of line under the curve of the hook and gave a quick jerk. The devil bug lay in my left hand.

After Doc got the good news, he said, "Now Jake, get Beth one more shot, and she will be ready for bed."

Over the next several minutes numerous radio calls offering congratulations crackled over Folsom's radio.

"Jake, next time I have to go under the knife, you're the man!"

"Beth, the hell with one shot, go for a double, you earned it, Babe!"

"Beth, you are one cool customer. No damn way would I let Jake near my eye!"

CHAPTER 25

◇◇◇

Maine's Crown Jewel—Ablaze!

Forever-wild Baxter State Park was in flames. The Maine Forest Service urgently recruited men and equipment to fight the conflagration. Pilots were needed to fight the flames from the air, and when I arrived at Folsom's Air Service shortly after sunrise to volunteer, people were already coming and going.

In Maine, before 1960, forest fires were fought by men carrying five-gallon Indian tanks on their backs and driving military surplus four-wheel-drive trucks. The vehicles transported high-pressure pumps to ponds or streams, and long lengths of linen hose were laid through the woods to a fire. Then a better idea came along.

Dick Folsom, in conjunction with The Maine Forest Service, modified his DeHavilland Beaver to pick up 120 gallons of lake water while taxiing at high speed. To accomplish this, two scoops were secured to the float hull, extending just below the waterline. Pipes connected the scoops to a large, bullet-shaped tank mounted between the pontoons. Two sealed doors were fitted to the bottom of the tank. A mechanism was designed to open and close the bottom doors from the pilot seat. Thus, a large volume of water, traveling forward at sixty miles an hour, could be aimed at a blaze. The plane could fill the reservoir in ten seconds, fly to the fire, and dump the water in one second. Eventually, the State bought five military-surplus

Beavers from the army and equipped them in a similar manner.

All five were soon inbound to Baxter. In addition, a large twin-engine CL215 from Canada was on the way. That aircraft could drop over 1000 gallons per load.

Flying near a large fire requires concentration. Thick smoke severely limits visibility, and rising hot air creates turbulence. In order to coordinate the movement of six planes, a command aircraft circles high overhead. Especially important are the positions of ground crews on foot. The water from a Beaver could injure a firefighter on impact, and the load from the Canadian monster could easily kill multiple men. The Beaver pilots were directed to pick up water in Hurd Pond, the closest safe spot near the fire. We formed a line, separated by enough distance so that only one aircraft was on the water at a time.

The technique required to scoop up water efficiently is as follows: upon touchdown, immediately add enough power so that the Beaver races along on top of the water but does not go airborne. Very quickly, the pilot feels a large drag as the tank fills. At that point, after eight seconds or so, full power is applied, and the airplane is wrestled off the surface. Between drag and load, the aircraft does not want to fly. After rotating one float out of the water, it will slowly gain speed and take to the air.

Dropping the load is all about timing. Since the water is traveling at the speed of the Beaver, it must be released somewhat before the target, in order to hit the mark. Water is released two or three hundred feet above the ground. A well-placed shot will quell a good-sized hot spot.

While we were water-bombing, the Forest Service established a fuel-and-maintenance depot on Togue Pond. Since the planes could only fly for three hours at a spell, refueling was needed often. By nightfall, a large mess tent, a command center, and first-aid station were in place. Several hundred workers had assembled to fight the out-of-control blaze. Trucks and bulldozers were parked everywhere. With several fuel breaks, we dropped water until dark. By this time, the front surfaces of the Beavers were jet-black from soot. Motel rooms were reserved by the State for the night; exhausted, and still feeling the vibration of flight all through my frame, a bed was a most welcome sight.

Early the following morning, after breakfast in the mess tent, pilots warmed the radial engines and took to the sky. The blaze had intensified, and whole mature fir trees were exploding like torches. The fire raced from treetop to treetop faster than a man could run. After a couple of hours, a desperate call came over the radio.

"All Beaver pilots, this is Forestry Command One, urgent, urgent, urgent. Repeating, all Beaver pilots, this is Forestry Command One, urgent, urgent, urgent.

"A crew of at least six is surrounded by flames and retreating down Abol Stream. They are extremely hot. Immediately, repeat, immediately, all pilots drop water on the men from 200 feet above the trees, no lower, repeat no lower!"

"CL215 pilot, this is Forestry Command One, urgent, urgent, urgent. You will not, repeat not, drop any water on the crew. Your heavy load could easily kill the men. Confirm message."

"Forestry Command One, CL215 roger that, will not drop water on crew."

The object was to create a rain to control temperature. I remember looking down and seeing desperate faces. My stomach was in a knot because the situation appeared hopeless. On some passes the men were obscured by plumes of flame and smoke. I never before had watched anyone slowly die.

After what seemed to be an hour, a miracle occurred.

"All Beaver pilots, this is Forestry Command One. Resume normal operations. Job well done. Everyone is safe."

By day three, a couple of thousand acres of woodland had burned, and no end was in sight. Perhaps our efforts were slowing the advance, but everyone knew that Mother Nature had the upper hand.

"Forestry Command One, Max here."

"Max, Forestry Command One, go."

"Yeah, for what it's worth we could make a lot more drops by picking up in the river at Abol. There's plenty of room."

"Max, Forestry Command One, permission granted. Only Max will pick up from the river."

Max swung toward the Penobscot and easily picked up a load. Permission followed for all. The complicating factor was that we had to land, negotiate a gradual bend, and then pick up the water. Everyone adjusted, and much collective time was saved. As I approached the river to land, my eye was on the plane ahead. The pilot landed perfectly, but carried too much speed into the bend. The Beaver skidded across the water and impacted the bank.

The event lasted only a few seconds, but I remember the scene frame-by-frame: the plane skipping sideways in a series of short hops; the wing striking the embankment; the plane rotating around the wingtip and slamming into the trees. Since the fuselage was undamaged and the pilot wore a military harness, I was not concerned about an injury to my friend. I aborted my landing.

It turned out that an AP reporter had begged a ride in the water-bomber to take close-up photos of the blaze. Through the front windshield, the photographer snapped a shot seconds before the crash that clearly showed approaching tree limbs. Luckily, no one was injured for that iconic image that was printed the next day in newspapers across the country.

Finally, heavy rain knocked down the Baxter fire. Crews worked until snowfall extinguishing underground smokes. Over 4000 acres were consumed.

For several years the area of the fire looked like a rocky desert. The blaze was so hot that the top soil had combusted. The exposed boulders appeared to have been sowed by a giant hand. But after time passed, the vegetation grew higher than the rocks, and the scar morphed into a green field when viewed from afar. Today a new forest, without memory of the trauma, covers the site.

But when I occasionally pass that way, my mind drifts back to 1978. What a demonstration of power by Mother Nature! All of the firefighters—using planes, bulldozers, and high-pressure pumps—were nearly useless. That fire ended only when Mother said, "Enough!"

CHAPTER 26

◇◇◇

The Strangest Flight of All

The following tale may strike the reader as far-fetched. Trust me, all of these events occurred during one round-trip journey.

As more and more customers discovered Hardscrabble, we out grew the trusty Supercub. Many times I almost purchased a larger floatplane, but then backpedaled from the deal. Dick Folsom came across a four-passenger Aeronca Sedan fitted with a 180-horsepower engine. The 1949 plane had been restored, and sat on almost-new Edo 2000 floats. The asking price was more than fair. Dick had used this type of aircraft during the 50s and 60s, and assured me that, with the more powerful motor installed, the Aeronca would really perform. He and I flew to Culpepper, Virginia during the winter to scrutinize the machine.

I wrote a deposit check, and agreed to fly the floatplane back to Maine as soon as the lake melted. When Albert, the owner of the Sedan, found out that Dick was brokering a beat-up Cessna 180 amphibian for a bargain price, he jumped at the opportunity. That stroke of luck meant I could fly the old Cessna to Culpepper and return in the Sedan.

The old amphibian was owned by an even older judge, named Paul, from New Hampshire. Paul had flown for decades, and was a regular visitor to Greenville. He was one of the most eccentric, entertaining individuals I had ever known. Paul was a legendary public official.

Once when Dick visited his courtroom for a morning, the judge listened to testimony in a complicated commercial contract dispute. Paul rendered a judgment just before noon, and then said, "I want to ponder appropriate damages over lunch." During the meal he asked Dick what he thought about the decision. Dick proceeded to explain why he felt the conclusion was dead wrong. After eating, Paul returned to the courtroom and reversed his judgment. Another time, an insolent teenager stood before the bench smirking and avoiding eye contact. At 70, the good judge vaulted the barrier, put his face in the teen's face and warned, "If you are not back here tomorrow morning, cleaned up, and respectful, you will rot in jail." That did the trick!

Paul crashed about half a dozen airplanes. Once he had lain on his back on the ice all night; another time he was stranded in the crown of a large maple tree for hours. The judge enjoyed showing a compilation movie documenting the aftermath of each wreck.

In March, Carl and I left Greenville and headed to Manchester, New Hampshire to pick up Paul. The Cessna 180 had been at Folsom's in order to render it safe for the flight. The cabin smelled of cigar smoke and car gas.

When I opened the pilot's door, Paul was standing in the taxi area eager to go.

"Jake, my good man, great to see you again. Jump right out of that cream puff so I can climb in and give you a few pointers on the way to the Confederacy! You think the old wreck has a couple more hours of life left?"

"Paul, you sure you want to push your luck? I'll be glad to keep flying."

"Get your ass out of that seat! I've delivered every plane I've sold. Come to think of it, in the case of several planes, I made that last flight period!"

"Paul, you are the only man I know who loves to joke about his crashes!"

I was not happy; now I'd have to carefully watch his every move. Some of the instruments were broken. At one point Paul flew an incorrect heading until I reminded him that the directional gyro had frozen.

After three hours, we needed gas.

"Reading tower, Cessna 456 Charlie, Charlie." No response.

"Reading tower, Cessna 456 Charlie, Charlie." No response.

"Reading tower, Reading tower, do you read Cessna 456 Charlie, Charlie?"

"Paul, just like every other part of this junk, your radio is worthless. Let's go on and land at an uncontrolled field."

"Jake, I learned a long time ago not to fear the Feds. I'll just fly the pattern and wait for light signals."

"Okay, you're the pilot, but you're asking for trouble. The last thing we need is for the FAA to inspect this thing!"

We circled the field and waited for light signals (towers have red and green spotlights for emergencies). A small jet was parked on the end of the runway, but had not moved the entire time. The undulating grass behind it confirmed that the engines were alive.

After ten minutes, no signal had appeared.

"Lazy bastards, probably just sitting there drinking coffee. I'm not waiting any longer. The hell with 'em!"

"Paul, no way can we just overfly a running airplane on an active runway!"

Paul quipped, "The FAA works for us; we don't work for them."

As the floatplane roared over the sleek jet, I read on the fuselage: "United States of America." Bad news! We had overflown one of the president's fleet of aircraft.

"Paul, you are screwed big time! Did you read the lovely words down the side of that jet?"

For once, Paul was silent!

Soon a car appeared with a large sign mounted on the roof. On it in large letters were the two words, FOLLOW ME. We were escorted to the base of the tower and ushered inside. Paul lit a cigar.

The supervisor (middle-aged, grossly overweight, and outfitted in a cheap suit) stated, "You just landed in a controlled airport without permission."

The judge stepped up and replied, "I've been flying for 50 years, and never before have I encountered a tower crew who ignored a constantly circling airplane. You are required by regulation to give us a light signal. If you don't want us to land, the color is red, my good man. What is your federal badge number?"

"Umm, umm. I'll let you off with a warning," the supervisor said, obviously taken aback.

After fueling up and several more hours of flying, Culpepper was just ahead. I dreaded the upcoming landing. The runway was short and narrow. On approach, Paul was performing well, but my hands were inches away from the yoke. He stalled several feet above the pavement. We slammed down.

Not a word was uttered.

After climbing out, I noticed a flame tube protruding from the muffler. That circular metal can is normally welded inside the structure. I kept my mouth shut!

Albert, the buyer, circled his new prize, and was instantly attracted to the defect.

"What the hell is this?"

Paul examined the muffler and declared, "Never noticed that before, must have happened on the flight down." He agreed to pay for the part.

Truth was, we hit hard enough to dislodge the tube!

At least I would fly from now on. Early the next morning, Carl and I headed north in the Sedan. What a gem! The old girl flew beautifully and had power to spare. Since Carl had grown up on the eastern shore of Maryland, we detoured slightly to overfly his childhood stomping grounds on the Sassafras River. I enjoyed seeing the landscape Carl spoke of so often.

Over Delaware, huge thunderheads materialized. We landed in the Delaware River, and tied the Sedan off to the shore. Industrial plants surrounded the banks. After an hour, the air ahead was clear. We flew up the Jersey Shore, by the Statue of Liberty and docked at Little Ferry, New Jersey. A long day was behind us, but all had gone well. The attendant topped off the fuel tanks.

A diner, a short walk away on a nearby traffic circle, was highly recommended for a meal. Waitresses delivered plates lined up along their arms just like on television. On the walls were numerous enlarged photographs of a smiling lady wiping different counters. Turns out, the Bounty paper-towel commercials were filmed at that location. After a satisfying meal, Carl, Paul, and I wandered across the rotary in the direction of a motel.

Expensive cars were parked about, but the place seemed dead.

"Jake, something is weird here. Limos are everywhere, but that immense lobby is empty and the lights are off!"

The door was unlocked, so we went inside. No one stood behind the front desk. Paul rang the bell. After a moment, an unusually attractive woman appeared.

I volunteered to speak for our group. "Hi, we just flew into the seaplane base and need two rooms for one night."

She seemed puzzled. "Just a second." Then she was gone.

In a couple of minutes the girl returned, smiled and said, "Far as I can find out, you are welcome to stay."

We did stay, but sensed something was unusual. The rooms were first-class. We learned at breakfast the next morning that we had interrupted a mob function. We may have been among the few paying guests ever. Our older waitress just laughed when we inquired.

The next morning we flew up the Hudson River just off the water. The World Trade Center towers loomed skyward to the right. Directly below was the future location of "The Miracle on the Hudson" (where the Airbus 320 crash landed in the Hudson River but everyone survived). Up the river, West Point was perched on the shore.

As Maine crept underneath, open water ponds vanished. I knew of a lake in the Waterville area that usually melted early. We left the Sedan tied to the shore, and Beth came with transportation to Greenville. Two weeks later, I completed the round trip to Moosehead Lake, content with a floatplane that would last us until we sold Hardscrabble.

CHAPTER 27

◊◊◊

Mutiny on the East Branch

Chuck was a great friend who had pioneered recreational raft trips down Maine's wildest rivers: the Kennebec, the West Branch of the Penobscot, and the Dead. He was also the consummate promoter. During the previous winter, he had booked over 100 adventurers to run the East Branch of the Penobscot, a new experience for Chuck and his guides. After flying the length of the river the previous summer, he welcomed a new challenge.

In late March, after snowmelt had begun, Chuck asked me to pick him up at Rockwood, on Moosehead Lake, and proceed to fly the river to see what shape it was in, post-winter. I was still flying on skis because the ice was solid. We flew north to Grand Lake Mattagamon, and followed the river course. Water levels were high, and floating ice chunks moved rapidly in the current. Chuck was pleased. As we progressed, the river channel was clearly defined, although ice dams blocked the flow in a couple of locations.

After half an hour, the river transformed. Banks were submerged, and water overflowed the land to a width of 500 feet in places. Trees and shrubs protruded from the water, and hundreds of dead-end coves were formed by the vegetation.

"We are screwed!" Chuck said. "From raft level, this meandering channel's not going to be seen, and because of the extreme width of the flooding, hardly any current is going to be flowing."

I flew that stretch back and forth several times as he made notes. Then we flew back to Rockwood. It was too late to cancel the trip. In fact, many customers had given their money at The Sportsman Shows, and Chuck only had names, no addresses.

I ran into Chuck later in the summer, and he recounted a horror story.

The large party, filling many rafts, each with a guide, had departed very early in the morning. The rafting company had restocked the emergency kits with two fresh flashlights, the guides had secure compasses, and a hearty lunch was onboard for each guest. The first several hours of the float went smoothly. The pace was rapid, and many waterfalls provided thrills, while some bordered on frightening. That was exactly the recipe for a successful day. Then the current began to ebb. The channel was still obvious, but the surrounding land was slightly flooded. After another hour, they essentially encountered a lake. Now, everyone had to paddle in order to maintain decent speed.

Which fork to take? The group was confronted with a maze. The rafts huddled together while the most experienced guides, including Chuck, made decisions. Chuck consulted his notes, as they often helped clarify a direction. But his impression from the air had been accurate. No obvious route was visible. Everyone charged ahead, paddling away. Several times the rafts had to reverse course after arriving at a dead end. The guests began to tire rapidly from exertion, and some started complaining.

"This is not what we signed up for!"

"I'm getting eaten alive!"

The slow pace allowed black flies and mosquitoes to attack the throng. Not everyone had repellent. And then the worst! Darkness fell. The flashlights came out to light the way. Obstacles were even more confusing in the dark. A full-scale mutiny threatened, but there was no way to leave.

After midnight the crew reached the pick-up point. No one had eaten since lunch. Most rafters were wet and swollen with insect bites. Some had completely lame arms. Ahead was a two-hour school-bus ride back to the cars.

Chuck told me that was the worst day of his life. Never again did he book a trip on a river without a trial run. I offered to take him for a return aerial tour. He declined.

CHAPTER 28

◇◇◇

Mooseburgers, Anyone?

Sometime during the summer of 1980, Connie called in on Folsom's radio and asked for Beth.

"Beth, is your real name Mary Elizabeth Morrel?" she inquired.

"Yes," Beth confirmed.

"Well, Beth, you have been selected for a permit to hunt moose. Congratulations!"

That was like winning the lottery! Tens of thousands had applied that first year for the 700 permits issued.

Maine Inland Fish and Wildlife had scheduled the season for the last week of September, a convenient time for us. Mid-September, we flew our area looking for a small bog with signs of moose activity. A promising candidate near Tom Fletcher Pond was our first choice.

Regrettably, Mother Nature did not cooperate with the State schedule. The last week in September was unseasonably hot. Noontime temperatures soared above 90. Hunting was uncomfortable, and worse, the preservation of tender moose meat would be a great challenge. All of the local stores ordered extra ice. The State brochure recommended rubbing pepper on the exposed section of the carcass to discourage blowflies.

Beth was a very relaxed huntress. She packed several books to read while sitting in a concealed spot near the bog. I sat directly behind her and did not read. Within a couple of hours, I spotted movement in the alder bushes next to the water. Soon, a good-sized cow stepped out and slowly ambled along broadside. Beth continued reading. I touched her elbow gently, and she turned. My index finger signaled toward the moose. My wife shouldered her rifle, and then lowered the firearm.

"I just can't shoot a sitting duck. You do it," she whispered.

The bolt action 30-06 was an accurate weapon. After a loud crank rang out, the cow's legs folded.

Since our objective was harvesting a year's worth of meat, time was critical. We were 1000 feet from our pickup, parked on a small logging road. I field-dressed the animal, and separated the carcass into four quarters. Each probably weighed almost two hundred pounds. Sweat poured off my body.

Next, I headed toward the truck in order to find a skidder operator. Skidders are immense machines with seven-foot-diameter tires, able to haul several trees at a time over stumps and large rocks. From our perch on the bog, we had heard a machine to the north. Once in the truck, I slowly drove in that direction looking for the harvesting area.

The operator was approaching a log yard when I arrived. He was French and spoke only broken English. I pretended to raise a gun to my shoulder, yelled "bang!" and held out a fifty-dollar bill. He comprehended immediately, and motioned for me to climb up into the cab. Skidders do not have two seats. I clung to the protective roll cage.

Loggers are always in a hurry. Their paycheck is based on production. Soon, the gigantic tires were bouncing over stumps and fallen trees as we crossed the clearing. My hands tired from squeezing the cage. Finally, the bog came into view.

The two of us hoisted high each chunk of moose and secured it to the skidder log arch. Then I had to endure one more trip!

When the meat was loaded in the pickup, we struck for Rockwood to buy ice.

Beth kept turning around and looking through the cab rear window at the meat.

"Jake, that's disgusting! There are hundreds of blowflies crawling over our future dinner! How do they hold on at 50 miles per hour?"

With a dozen bags of ice packed around our winter meat, we raced for Greenville. A local butcher had volunteered his walk-in cooler. Beth and I spent the next day helping the meat cutter process the trophy. (I decided to buy an industrial meat grinder someday.) As expected, the meat we ate that winter was better than the best beef.

The following year, Burt and I were ready to head into Hardscrabble to slaughter the pigs and prepare for hunting season. Over drinks, I was killing time, leafing through our local six-page paper. In the classified section, a meat grinder was listed for sale—asking price $150. Burt and I decided to take a chance and drive up and take a look the next morning before departing.

The grinder turned out to be industrial all right! Together, Burt and I could barely lift the monster. The owner knew little about it, and since the machine was wired for 220V, we could not test it. I offered $100, which was accepted.

After hunting season, I cleaned and inspected my latest toy. For a 1930s machine, the condition was excellent. Plus, the thing was built like a tank! When plugged into the correct outlet, it purred.

Beth went downtown and bought some sirloin to test the machine. She cut the meat into two inch cubes, and dropped a couple down the chute.

"Unbelievable!" Beth said, thrilled. The machine sucked the offering down in seconds. "That would have taken five minutes with the old hand grinder."

"Watch your fingers," I replied.

Word spread around Greenville that Jake owned a monster

grinder. Neighbors in a small town know who have useful heavy machines, especially needed in wintertime when moose frequent the roads. They crave the salt spread after snowstorms, and unfortunately, many are hit and killed. Maine wardens normally give the meat to the person with the demolished car. Many times we received requests to grind mooseburger, and customarily, part of the meat was offered in payment.

So, for years, the $100 dollars earned interest. Our family enjoyed the best of steak and roasts, and Bullwinkle stew was my favorite meal.

CHAPTER 29

◇◇◇

Frozen In—a Long Way from Home

During the ten days of the Harrisburg Sportsman Show, it became traditional for exhibitors to gather at various local restaurants late in the evenings. Over drinks and dinner, we discussed common problems and different solutions, and Beth and I met some interesting people. Luke and Pauline, for instance, operated a lodge located on a royal lease in the wilderness north of Ottawa. We became great friends, and often sat at the same table during group gatherings. One year, Luke had a proposition.

"Why don't you and Carl fly up for a few days? We can exchange favors. You stay free, then fly me around my lease—it's huge, and I haven't gotten to check on the most remote cabins. What do you say?"

A topographical map of the lease showed as much water as land: lakes and ponds everywhere. The native guides transported the sports to the outpost camps by crossing lakes and portaging to the next water body, repeatedly. Sometimes, the better part of a day was required. Because of time constraints, Luke had been unable to visit some of his cabins for years. He was worried that many needed work. Using my floatplane, we could tour all of them in a couple of days.

October was the only month when we could leave Hardscrabble, and that worked well for Luke. On the day of departure, I had agreed to fly a fisherman to Munsungan Lake, an hour north of Greenville. Spotty ground-fog hugged the land along the route. I worried that the fog would thicken, making a landing at the Bradford Camps impossible. Luck smiled on Munsungan. Ninety percent of the water was obscured, but a beautiful, sunny spot stood out on the far side. We landed and taxied through the fog, by compass, to the dock. Dave, the owner, was amazed to see a floatplane materialize out of the soup. Departure was far easier, since the layer was only a couple of hundred feet deep. Five seconds after takeoff, I saw the sun, and took a course for Greenville.

Carl had our dunnage stacked on the dock. I fueled, loaded, and blasted off. The weather was forecast to deteriorate, but since the route mostly followed wide rivers we were not concerned.

At Lac Megantic, a landing for customs was necessary. Canadian customs officials are polite. When I killed the engine adjacent to the large pier, he called, "Do you have any firearms?"

My answer, "No."

The reply, "Enjoy Canada!"

Off to the Saint Lawrence River. Now we transformed into a fast boat. The river is so wide that flying 100 feet high was easy. A right-hand turn led into the Ottawa River. Again, easy low-altitude navigation. The clouds were lowering, so the rivers were a godsend. The fuel gauges indicated one quarter when the City of Ottawa loomed ahead. Unfortunately, the seaplane base had closed for the summer. We tied to shore. Packed in the baggage compartment were two 5-gallon tanks. The Cessna held almost sixty gallons of fuel. By walking repeatedly to the adjacent land airport, filling two five gallons cans and then returning, slowly the plane tanks were filled. As a safety measure, we stowed the two full 5-gallon tanks as well.

The Gatineau River led north from Ottawa. The weather was worse. Up the river, filled with logs headed to the mills, we ventured. As darkness approached and drizzle began, Maniwaki lay ahead, our destination for the night.

Carl and I decided to visit a local bar for a beer. After seating ourselves and ordering, we relived the day. While sipping away, I noticed that every other person in the place was from a native tribe.

When the bartender, a rugged native woman, brought the next beers, she commented, "Are you waiting for others to join?"

"No, there are just two of us."

"Okay, I just thought perhaps others were waiting for you upstairs. That's the white bar. You're welcome to stay if you want."

We did. (Interesting to note how politely she spoke to us, but not to her regulars. At one point she dragged a passed-out native girl across the room and out to the sidewalk!)

Weather was first-class the next morning, and the flight farther north to Lac McArthur was uneventful. We were a long way from home. The fir and spruce trees were stunted, with a few birches mixed in. Water bodies predominated between ribbons of land. The topography was flat.

Luke and I spent two days inspecting camps. Some broke his heart.

"Jake, why didn't I get you up here when we first met? I can't believe that my guests haven't complained. What a horror! Makes me feel like shit! Tomorrow I will radio out and try to find a full time handyman."

Snowflakes floated in the air late that afternoon. A warning was announced by the radio telephone operator. "A storm is imminent for this evening."

All night the wind howled, and the temperature dropped. We checked on the plane, and removed accumulated snow from the tail. A heavy snow load on the tail can sink a floatplane. The following day was the same—no let-up.

"According to the aviation weather information service, the storm will be over in 24 hours," said Luke. "The bad news is that the next blizzard is coming in two days."

"Luke, we have to leave immediately after the storm. If we delay, the plane could be trapped all winter. That could ruin it!"

When we stepped outside, morning had dawned only cloudy. But a problem was immediately apparent.

"Oh, man, the lake's frozen over," I said to Carl.

Luke and I plotted a solution over breakfast.

"Jake, my 18-foot workboat will break that ice. She's rugged and heavy, with a 25 Mercury. The three of us can drag her to the shore and shove her out on the ice. When we climb aboard, I'm betting the ice will break. With the bow high, the motor will keep breaking out a channel."

"Sounds like a plan, Luke. We can shove the broken pieces under the main sheet so they won't damage the floats. The sides of the pontoons are less than 0.025 inches thick (a little thicker than a credit card). One hole and we're dusted!"

It took several hours to break up a narrow opening long enough for takeoff, but finally everyone said goodbye as the engine idled for a long time. An airplane engine must be thoroughly warm for maximum performance. The available takeoff distance was limited, we were heavy, and full power was a must. Once we were accelerating on top of the water, I knew the old girl would fly. Just before the end of our ice-chopped runway, we leapt into the sky headed for Greenville.

The trip home was the mirror of the trip up, including carrying gasoline tanks in Ottawa. We cleared American customs in Jackman. The agent was much more curious than his counterpart, but let us in. Greenville was a welcome sight.

CHAPTER 30

◇◇◇

Beth Smacks a Bobcat

During March, in our old farmhouse in Greenville, most evenings we received reservation calls for the upcoming fishing season. I boiled maple syrup and processed next year's firewood simultaneously. When the weather was ideal, we made the first skiplane runs into Hardscrabble. March was the last relaxing month until after hunting season in the fall.

During late winter, wild animals that normally never visit appear around small villages. Hunger drives them to find sources of food when their prey becomes scarce. Every few days, the local press reports a sighting. Bobcats are common visitors.

I was not present for part of the following saga, but Beth has recounted the story many times.

My wife has keen ears, much better than mine. Late one afternoon she heard a strange noise in the ell of the old farmhouse, which leads to the woodshed. She knew in a heartbeat that our beloved cat Krispy was in distress. Beth flew out the door, and was confronted by a desperate situation. A bobcat had his jaws around Krispy's head. Without thinking, my wife grabbed the nearest weapon, which was a broom, and charged the large feline.

The bobcat took one look at the furious female headed his way and panicked. Clawing its way up the wall next to Beth, the animal jumped over her shoulder and dove behind our chest freezer.

Poor Krispy was hurting. His head was punctured in several

places, but he was breathing. Beth rushed him into the house and called me. I was working on our Supercub at Folsom's when Connie got the call. I rushed home while Beth took off for the vet's, 30 miles away.

When I looked behind the freezer, bobcat eyes stared back. I called the local warden, who rushed over. Unfortunately, the cat escaped before Charlie arrived. He let me know that several of my neighbors had reported sightings of the beast.

Two days later, all of my neighbor's ducks were killed inside the duck house. His hired man became suspicious when he discovered that the small propped duck door had fallen. Looking in the window, he saw the slaughtered ducks AND the trapped bobcat. Sam cracked the window and shot the animal with a pistol.

Sam's boss, a wealthy, retired gentleman farmer, decided to have the cat mounted. He took the carcass to the local taxidermy shop. When I heard about the chain of events, I called Fred (the taxidermist and a friend). He agreed to let us photograph the trophy. In that picture, Beth who stands 5 feet, 2 inches, holds the critter's head next to her head while the paws reach the ground. The animal was emaciated, weighing about 25 pounds.

Our veterinarian said the large predator was just playing with our cat. He explained that with jaws powerful enough to break a deer's neck in one bite, the bobcat could have killed Krispy in a flash. Other than a dose of antibiotics, no treatment was possible. Our cat laid next to the woodstove for days, while Beth encouraged him to lick tuna oil off her finger. I knew he would not make it.

Then one morning, Krispy's bed was empty. He had gotten to his feet and walked over to the feeding bowl. That great pet lived many more years.

Beth and I talked many times about the fact that the predator could have killed her as easily as a deer. I can only assume she put the fear of God into the animal. Don't mess with Beth!

CHAPTER 31

◇◇◇

After Climbing Out of the Cockpit, They High-five

(This story falls into the category of, "Yeah, tell me another one!" Again, all is true—I watched the events unfold with my own eyes.)

Randall and Sue flew into Hardscrabble several times a year. The two of them had constructed a Volmer flying boat, and enjoyed flying to Maine and relaxing at Spencer Lake. After the wheels were lowered, the amphibian taxied out of the water onto the beach.

Randall, a nuclear engineer, worked for himself. His specialty was stress analysis of power-plant components during earthquakes. Before supercomputers, he had combined smaller computers in parallel to create a very fast processor. Still, calculations took days. Our guest was the only subcontractor engaged in this niche market at that time. Contracts were infrequent, but extremely lucrative. The couple had a lot of spare time.

During the winter, they lived on Crooked Island in the Bahamas, an hour and a half by plane, south of Nassau. The natives of Crooked embraced a relaxed lifestyle. They speared fish, grew small gardens (referred to as farms), and raised children communally. A workweek was unknown. Because Randall had a plane and many tools, he became the "go-to man" on the Crooked. He loved solving challenges.

Year after year, Sue begged Beth to convince me to visit them during the winter. Since Thea and Zeke were rapidly becoming more independent, we finally made the trip. At Nassau, a reggae band played inside the terminal. It was hot! Our host was waiting as promised, and his winter plane, a Bonanza V-tail, was just outside. This, of course, was before 9/11. (Before 9/11, Folsom's could fly customers to Bangor, Maine, taxi up to a jet, and discharge the passengers next to the plane's stairs!)

We soon were headed south, flying about 1000 feet high. The shallow water on the United States' side of the islands was a beautiful shade of light blue. Total clarity allowed a view down to the coral reefs. Shipwrecks were visible in startling detail. Surprisingly, we also saw plane after plane sitting in the shallows. Some of the larger aircraft, such as DC-3s, protruded above the surface.

"Almost all of the wrecks were drug planes," explained our host. "They were landed intentionally "wheels up" in the shallow water. When the pilot skims in on top of the water, the plane partially sinks. One drug haul is worth many times the cost of the old plane. The natives don't use drugs, but they count on the fees they earn from transferring waterproof drug bales to shore. They use small boats."

"If you know about this, don't the police?"

"The Bahamian law enforcement ignore this activity."

"Maybe a kickback situation?"

"Who knows…"

We flew by a huge blimp tethered to the land by a massive, long cable. This landmark belonged to The United States Drug Enforcement Agency. Intelligence gleaned from the blimp was fed to Black Hawk helicopters, which zipped along everywhere.

Crooked Island had an adequate gravel strip within walking distance of the couple's cottage. Randall greased the plane onto the short runway, and our vacation in paradise commenced.

Randall was an accomplished spear fisherman, so we dined on

rock lobster and numerous local species of fish. We explored endless white beaches by boat, and entered several small, grown-up inlets in order to reach deserted plantation ruins.

On the third day, a native came bearing an urgent message.

"A sailor on a charter boat is badly sunburned and needs to be flown to the hospital in Nassau. Can you make the trip?"

"Of course," Randall said, and we were soon airborne on the way to Mayaguana Island to pick up the suffering man.

As we approached the old missile base, Randall spoke over the intercom. "Jake, I know this is hard to believe, but we may see some native boys flying near the strip. I'm not sure how it all started, but apparently one older teenager somewhere learned just enough to take off and land, after a fashion. He taught the others as much as he knows. If we see them, we'll give them a wide berth because they all are an accident waiting to happen."

"Really, Randall? That's the most outrageous story I've ever heard. You can't be serious! If your tale is true, I'd do anything to watch!"

When the long runway was dead ahead, Randall pointed and exclaimed, "Look at that plane taking off!"

The plane swerved left and right as it gained speed. Once in the air, it porpoised up and down while drifting from side to side. While we stayed out of the way, the pilot made a big, slow circle and approached to land. The aircraft hit hard initially, bounced several times, then slid to a stop at an angle to the runway. We landed behind, and quickly turned off onto a taxiway. The two boys in the plane jumped out and slapped hands, high-fiving each other! Next, they reversed seats and repeated the same saga.

I was now a believer! Luckily, the skies did not become a dangerous obstacle course, and the mercy flight to Nassau was uneventful.

CHAPTER 32

◇◇◇

Oscar Fights One More Battle

Poverty Flats Airfield in Hinckley, Maine, was typical of thousands of small airports in rural America during the post-WWII decades. Twenty 1940s vintage small planes were tied down on either side of a narrow grass-and-dirt runway, surrounded by farm fields. However, the somewhat shabby appearance at first glance belied the fact that the strip was a busy place. Local residents would park along the country road next to the field most summer evenings, and watch planes come and go until dark. And once a month, the pilots and neighbors would gather for a homemade feast followed by a guest speaker.

After one of these memorable feeds, I met Cecelia Piper, a minister from the coastal town of Addison, Maine. Her transformation at normal retirement age stretches belief. Here's what had happened in her life…

Sitting on her porch along the bold coast of Down East, Maine, Cecelia could barely make out the neighbor's home 200 feet distant, but she could hear snippets of panicked conversation coming from the water. She made her way to the ocean, carrying a handheld gas-powered horn. Several blasts of the horn were answered, and soon a large sailboat emerged from the gloom with one frightened family from New York on deck. They explained that the fog bank had enveloped the boat almost instantly, dropping visibility to zero. After securing the yacht, Cecelia and the family hurried across the street to thaw out around the woodstove.

When decent weather returned, after a night in a comfortable bed and a couple of filling meals, the family prepared to leave. As a parting promise, the father told Cecelia that if she ever needed anything for her small parish to please call him without hesitation.

As the days passed, Cecelia became convinced that she had been called to care for the natives of rural Alaska. On a lark, she made that call and tried to explain her unusual vision. The yacht owner told her to please make a list of what she needed, and to also recommend a donation amount.

That is how Cecelia ended up near New York, learning to fly a brand-new Cessna 170, which could be fitted with wheels or floats or skis. She learned to fly, flew to Alaska, and spent her retirement helping the natives.

After many years, I ran into Cecelia under a different set of circumstances. During the mid-1980s I regularly flew lobsters from Millbridge, Maine, to Moosehead Lake, where my wife and I operated a lakeside restaurant. Initially, Linden Perry, a lobsterman, sold directly to me—right off the boat. Linden served as my weatherman on the scene, and always selected a sheltered cove for our rendezvous. By lashing the bow of the airplane floats onto the stern of the lobster boat, we easily transferred 300 pounds of the delectable critters, and I could make a quick getaway before the fog bank shifted. As time went on, Linden could not supply enough 1½-pound lobsters, so he sent me to Looks Pound in South Addison, just a skip away by air.

After securing my Cessna 180 to Look's float, I climbed the ladder, which bridged the large vertical distance between high and low tides. Standing there to greet me was none other than Cecelia Piper. We remembered each other, and quickly caught up. As I was about to leave to buy the lobsters, she asked me a favor.

"Jake, you probably have seen old Oscar sitting at his roll-top desk inside. He dresses in a suit every day, and comes to work in his old store. Oscar served in the Army Air Corps during the War in the Pacific, and I just know you could make his day by taking him on a flight. We often sit and talk when I come to shop. The war was hard on him, but he still loves to talk about planes."

"Cecelia, I think that is a great idea. Let's see if he'll go."

Slowly, Cecelia and I eased Oscar down the ladder to the float running along the wharf. I spun the plane around so he could clamber up over the struts on the passenger side and climb into the seat. After skimming across the harbor, the 180 was airborne, and Oscar's face lit up with the most genuine smile I could imagine. Fifteen minutes elapsed quickly, and since I never wanted to carry any extra weight during ocean takeoffs, my fuel time was limited. I asked Oscar if he wanted to view anything else.

"Yes, please fly low over Ship Stern Island."

Banking to the right and descending, we made for the island a few hundred feet above the water. As we approached the bluff face, Oscar slowly raised his large hands and lightly grasped the copilot's yoke. The noise he emitted was unmistakable: machine gun fire.

After a few seconds, Oscar turned to me and said in a soft voice, "I got every one of the bastards."

CHAPTER 33

◇◇◇

Call Humpy

Soon after I started flying at Folsom's Air Service, Dick Folsom introduced me to Humpy. Although his given name was Leonard, he was always Humpy, Humper or Hump to his friends.. He became both a best friend and mentor, demonstrating the fine points of everything from thin, walled-tubing welding to magneto repair. Humpy and I were thirty years apart in age, so I was fascinated by his childhood recollections. Many winter nights I sat next to his woodstove and listened to the tales.

For instance...during the Spanish flu epidemic of 1917, for months his father forbid anyone in the large family from leaving the farm. In addition, No-Trespassing signs were posted at the end of the farm lane...And...usually, Leonard and his siblings walked several miles to school, but sometimes in the winter traveled by sleigh.

But the life-and-death story that is seared into my brain took place because Humpy loved to trap in order to make pocket change. Stumbling over a log in the woods, a 25-caliber pistol discharged in his pocket. Blood oozed from his side on the way back to the farmhouse. His mother calmly moved a cot next to the parlor stove, lay Leonard down, and sent an older sibling to alert the country doc.

After a while he arrived, driving a single-horse carriage. Following an examination of Humpy, he announced his findings.

"Luckily, the bullet passed through a glove stashed in his pocket. The slug continued along the outside of the rib cage and is embedded in soft tissue below the armpit. Expect the wound to drain profusely. Change the dressings when soaked. Do not let the hole close. Expect a high fever, but still keep him warm. Expect severe pain. Hope, after a few days, the body ejects the lead."

One morning, after several days, the bullet lay on the cot!

Life really was less cushy years ago, and it's hard to imagine a high-school student today wanting to play basketball enough to travel the way Leonard had to, to get to the court. The winter schedule consisted of two round-robin tournaments staged in Houlton, Maine, a long train ride away. Humpy's father drove him to the train station. But no telephone lines had been strung in that part of Maine, and there was no way to alert the family upon his return. Leonard always walked the six miles back to the farm. Humpy surely had developed physical stamina from his family's lifestyle, and mental acuity was another strength he possessed.

Certain people's talents are so striking that respect for them never dies, though they might. By the time Humpy and I met, he was a legendary mechanic and airplane restorer. People all over Greenville went to Leonard for advice and assistance. Dick Folsom, a brilliant mechanic in his own right, once commented, "I've worked on airplanes since my days in The Army Air Force when the United States military approached Japan. Humpy is, by far, the most talented mechanic I have ever encountered. To top it off, he doesn't even have an FAA mechanic's license."

When I worked at Folsom's Air Service, Dick always employed at least one full-time mechanic. In addition, some pilots performed repairs under supervision. When our mechanic was stumped he would summon Dick, which usually led to a solution. When Dick was baffled, he always directed, "Call Humpy."

When Leonard arrived, he always sat in the office and talked with Connie for a spell before entering the shop. Dick would give a description of the problem. Then Leonard would inspect, think, and inspect some more without uttering a word. Finally, he always prefaced his opinion by saying, "I'm probably wrong, but try..." Rarely was he wrong!

One day a customer brought in a freshly overhauled engine that had seized up on the first test run. We disassembled the Lycoming, and laid the parts on clean sheets spread over the bench. Everything seemed perfect. "Call Humpy." After looking at each part carefully, Leonard went back into the office and continued talking with Connie. Finally, Dick couldn't stand it and asked what he thought.

"Dick, somebody has paired crankcase halves from two different engines. The serial numbers should always be consecutive. Those are not. However, I think it is possible to hand-scrape the two cases and solve the problem."

Nobody had ever heard of such a thing. But Humpy had worked on engines in the 1920s when the practice was common. Using 50-year-old hand tools, Leonard made that motor run like new.

Another day, on a supply run to Greenville, after flying Hardscrabble customers out in the morning, the aluminum surrounding the engine caught my eye. Watching carefully, I noticed that the engine was moving very slightly left and right with respect to the metal. Upon docking, I quickly removed the covering. Sure enough, a diagonal engine-mount brace was broken. Not good! Men in the woods, and no airplane! Folsom's did not have enough time to remove the motor, weld the tube, and reinstall the engine, so I could get back to the lodge and pick up the men. Call Humpy.

Soon Leonard arrived with a miniature Smith welding torch and several mirrors of various sizes. I was instructed to hold one mirror at a certain angle, while Humpy held a second in his left hand. Using the double reflection, he proceeded to backhand-weld the repair. Mirror inspection revealed a perfect bead. My guests ate dinner on time.

Exemplary skill, easy-going nature, and an appreciation for his life, makes Humpy a friend I'll never forget. One winter evening, while we sat next to the stove, Leonard reflected, "You know, I've lived in the best time period possible. When I was a boy, we got around using a horse and buggy. Today, I fly my floatplane anywhere I choose."

As my good friend was fading away, Dr. Fichtner put his hand on my shoulder and lamented, "What a shame to lose all that knowledge. I wish it was possible to gather the wisdom in my hand and sprinkle a little around to each of us. You know, if Leonard could have become a surgeon, he would have been a legend!"

Charlie Coe, the dean of floatplane pilots, flew Dick's DeHavilland Beaver to Leonard's funeral in Patten, Maine. The plane was full of present and former employees.

When we departed the service, just as Charlie swung toward Greenville, Jim, a mechanic, called out, "Charlie, lay one down on the Humper!"

That was all the former WWII P-51 pilot needed to hear. We turned in a slow circle back toward the cemetery and descended. Over the new grave, less than ten feet separated the floats of the Beaver from the coffin. "Here's to Humpy!" We all took a swig from our beers.

Suddenly, two people screamed, "Power lines!"

Less than 1000 feet ahead were high tension lines, and we were below them. Charlie advanced the throttle beyond 36 inches maximum power, to emergency over-boost. The PW-985 radial engine snorted and roared. Somehow, the Beaver was up to the task; or, did Humpy perform one last miracle?

CHAPTER 34

◇◇◇

Flying Over the Fen

As Beth and I aged, we yearned to experience other parts of the world. Given the fact that we had recently sold Hardscrabble, we felt a new sense of freedom. We had only traveled in the United States and visited Canada. Beth researched a trip to northern France lasting two weeks. We'd stay at inns in small villages and travel narrow, low-speed, rural roads. We would land in Paris and journey by train to Brest. From that point, we'd depart in a small rental car, thus avoiding the wild drivers of the big city.

Beth's plan was a great success. We stayed in beautiful, old stone buildings and were served meals prepared and presented in ways unknown to us. No ingredient was novel, but the appearance, taste, and combinations were a whole new world. The art form on the plate was so beautiful, I hated to take the first bite. We anticipated our evening meals all day long. Our goal was to reach Omaha Beach in Normandy after about ten days, then return to Charles de Gaulle Airport by train. Each day we wandered and explored, with no fixed itinerary.

Being an airplane nut, I bought a French aviation chart, and we stopped often at small, rural airports. The health of general aviation there was dismal. Fuel cost twice as much as in the United States. Also, most recreational VFR pilots were only allowed to fly in limited, designated areas adjacent to the home airport. As a result, most airfields were deserted. Near the walled city of Dinan, I begged a local pilot to give me a ride in order to lay claim to a flight over French soil. We struggled to take off in an underpowered Jodel and flew circles inside a triangle bounded by two rivers and a highway. So different from the freedom of unrestricted flight in Maine.

Finally, nearly to Omaha Beach, we pulled into an aerodrome where a couple had just landed in a Maule. Beth was furious, since she felt that I was too forward with strangers, but I still got out and introduced myself. Turned out they were English. Before 9/11, it was an easy matter to fly from England across the English Channel to France. John and Sue had a small farm, with an airstrip, in Ely, Cambridgeshire, a 30-minute flight from their summer cottage in France. We talked airplanes for 15 minutes, and I bid them good-bye and walked toward the car. Suddenly, Susan called, "Jake, would you and Beth consider joining us for dinner this evening?" We accepted in a heartbeat and agreed to meet at five.

John and Sue's cottage was located in a tiny village composed of about ten homes. The ancient, stone building had a thatched roof. We rode in their Citroen 2CV, the French farmer's car, along twisting, single-track roads that led to a castle with a restaurant. The owners knew our hosts well, and the four of us were seated in front of a massive stone fireplace with a six-foot opening. The meal was over the top. As an appetizer, we had translucent, thin scallop slices floating on seasoned olive oil. The following six courses were excellent, prepared using locally made cheeses, fresh eggs and produce, and recently slaughtered meats. Gorgeous melt-in-your-mouth desserts came last. Of course, French wine bottles cluttered the table. When we parted, John encouraged us to visit in England. I knew that would probably never happen, but promised we'd try.

Back in Greenville, I met an adventurous, can-do, English couple who had purchased an island camp on Moosehead Lake. Juliet and Charlie needed a part-time caretaker to open and close the buildings, a position Beth and I accepted. Over three years we became close friends, which led to an invitation to London. We agreed—so we would end up in Britain after all. Before leaving on the trip, having stayed in contact, I emailed John and Susan and received a reply demanding that we make a side trip to Ely.

After a few days in Barnes, we took a train from London to Cambridge. John and Susan met us at the station. Their picturesque farm was a short drive away. The next morning, John announced we were going flying. He had a WWII Piper L4, an observation plane, in a shed, and the two of us wheeled it out. John was the pilot. I was the rear-seat passenger. We spent the next couple of hours flying over eastern England at about 500 feet above the ground. Mostly, we were over the Fen, a level agricultural area which had been reclaimed from the sea.

Obviously, John held senior statesman status. Military controllers knew him by his first name. After he radioed, "I'm giving a Yank pilot a ride," they granted permission to roam at will. We overflew countless abandoned American airfields on the east coast. A new strip appeared every couple of miles. One of the Queen's summer castles lay below, as did the American pilot's cemetery. Ely cathedral was breathtaking.

"That church steeple is so high," said John, "it often protrudes from the fog layer in bad weather. During the War, returning pilots used the spire as a point of reference. It was a beacon, rising above a sea of white."

We stared at the charming scenery below.

"Guess how all the brown circles within the black farm fields came to be," John said.

I had no idea. "I'm stumped," I said.

"World War II bomb craters," said John. "When bombers returned with unused armament, it was dropped over the Fen before they landed. The soil used for fill was brown."

That evening we chatted airplanes while sipping John's single-malt scotch.

"Tomorrow's flight is going to be different," he said.

After breakfast, we were airborne again. This time, every 15 minutes or so, we landed at a small grass strip on a farm or estate. Sometimes, the "air strip" was really a manicured large front lawn, complete with formal plantings and gardens. At each location, wonderful people treated us to tea and biscuits. Many of his friends were older pilots with interesting World War II tales to share. We returned late in the day.

Those two days over England were the best flights of my life. I have often reflected on how lucky I was to have enjoyed such a unique, enjoyable experience.

CHAPTER 35

◇◇◇

Floatplane on the Sand

Folsom's Air Service extended so many favors to us during the summer that we were anxious to show how much we appreciated their kindness. We settled on hosting an annual fly-in party during mid-October. The crew, plus spouses and friends, were invited. We preheated the cabins, and Beth prepared a sumptuous evening meal and cooked breakfast for the wounded in the morning (there was always an open bar). Some years, half a dozen planes were parked at the lodge by evening.

One time I decided to climb the ridge above the camps to shoot some partridge for an hors d'oeuvre. My plan was to return when the first plane-engine sang in the distance. With two birds in hand, I heard it and walked rapidly to the lodge. The Cessna approached from the north, cut power, and landed. Shortly, a second plane did exactly the same thing. By this time, I could see the buildings through the trees. Just as I stepped out of the woods, a third airplane arrived from the north, circled, and set up a landing downwind from the *south*. The reason a plane lands into the wind is to reduce the touchdown speed. This craft, landing *with* the wind, was going to strike the water at a very high velocity! Something was wrong!

Occasionally, winds in the Spencer Lake gorge were hard to read from patterns on the water. A westerly breeze was sometimes deflected by the cliffs and appeared on the water to be blowing from both the north and south, in different parts of the lake. Experienced pilots kept track of the wind direction as they passed over each lake during a trip and were not fooled by a phantom wind. This pilot had been fooled and was in trouble. I ran the last 200 yards.

The Cessna was covering the remaining distance to the Hardscrabble shore too rapidly. It skipped off the water and landed in the lake only about 500 feet from shore, then raced out of the water onto the sand, sliding 100 feet and pivoting up over the nose of the float to nearly vertical. Fortunately, it settled back, right-side up, sitting on the floats. The scene was as if a giant crane had deposited the flying machine onto the beach.

As I raced to the door, the youngest Folsom stepped out, a teenager. He had commandeered an extra floatplane and invited two of his friends to the party. Both friends had been asleep and awoke when the plane was standing on its nose. What a way to wake up!

The pilot's first words were, "Is Dad here yet?" His second thought was, "We have to get this thing back in the water." His third question: "How many men are here?" Obviously, the kid could think on his feet.

As mentioned in earlier vignettes, Hardscrabble owned a 1953 Super C Farmall tractor. I fired the contraption up and drove to the plane. We attached two ropes to the float bows and raised the tractor bucket. The machine elevated the front, which was heaviest. Eight men lifted the rear of the floats, and collectively we could suspend the load for a few seconds at a time. So began the slow journey to the water. The tractor lifted and pushed simultaneously. When the men heaved upward, the airplane advanced a few feet. After a lot of sweat was shed, the landplane was again a seaplane.

"Okay, Junior, you owe us!" said one guy who'd done some of the hard labor. "Jake's handing out booze so you can't buy drinks, but you can lug 'em. I'll take an ice-cold Michelob. Twenty bucks and I won't spill the beans to your old man."

"You guys sure know how to kick a man when he's down. I looked at the wind but it changed during the approach."

"I don't think so, Bud! But I'll give you one thing: Spencer can be a mean place to land...Chalk it up to experience. Everything turned out okay."

We did not tell his father, Dick Folsom, about the incident when he arrived later that night. It did not seem right to spoil his evening. Later, I did speak up because I knew that the Cessna should be closely examined for internal structural damage. Taking care of Folsom's was the least I could do for Folsom's taking care of me.

EPILOGUE

◇◇◇

Reflections

Often, when Beth and I attend gatherings of friends with guests, a person we have known for years will introduce us with the quote, "Beth and Jake used to live in the woods of northern Maine." Almost always, the guest is intrigued and wants to know more. After we explain, this query usually follows: "My God, you two must really miss it. Why on earth did you sell?" The answer to that question is complex.

Do we have positive memories of Hardscrabble? You bet! Our first look at the dilapidated property, the warm feeling that maybe we could own a lodge, the burst when our meager offer was accepted by the heirs, mixed feelings when the bank granted our loan, pride when the old buildings were reconstructed, the thrill when customers responded at Sportsman shows, and ultimately the satisfaction when we were full of guests during the first week of operation. Also, of greater importance, was the joy of living and working with our children, Thea and Zeke.

So, was life at Hardscrabble just a pleasant dream? Definitely not! Would you do the same thing again? Definitely not! Are you happy you did it? You bet!

We accepted excessive risk to create our dream. The chance that we could rebuild an old set of cabins into a lodge and then recruit customers within a year was minuscule. Why the bank extended money, I have no idea! Our fortune, once we began operation, was on the line with every airplane flight. One mistake on my part, or one engine failure, could have doomed us, and worse, robbed my kids of their dad.

But the bottom line is that the world needs young people to take excessive risk, because older, more experienced adults usually won't. My life would be greatly diminished without the Folsom's people and all of our guests, who became close friends through flying. I am so glad we were headstrong and blundered ahead. Would I advise Thea and Zeke to go for it? I have, but only after a long discussion of how their mother and father were blessed with the best luck imaginable.

How did our experience running Hardscrabble impact our later years? Most significant: the successful completion of that huge project gave Beth and me the confidence to tackle other challenges. We rebuilt an old paper company warehouse on Moosehead Lake and established a successful lakeside restaurant called the H and W, gutted and restored an 1836 farmhouse in Greenville, moved a 40 by 60 foot barn on that same property, created a runway on Swans Island off the coast of Maine (and built a house nearby), and finally, designed and crafted our current home in Sangerville, Maine, located next to our grass air-strip.

I stated near the beginning of this book that "engineering was not for me." Obviously, that was a simplification. In fact, my education helped to plan numerous projects.

Beth and I are preparing for our forty-seventh wedding anniversary. We both feel that working together over the years contributed to our longevity as a couple. Once, as newlyweds, we learned to separate responsibilities and not meddle in each other's business, all went smoothly.

Do I miss flying every day, hunting twenty-five days a year, and fishing whenever the mood struck? Frankly, no! Great mental pressure accompanied those flights because often conditions were far from ideal. Today a Supercub-type airplane sits in the hangar next to our house. Most clear, calm mornings, I take a lazy 15-minute flight and enjoy looking down. Hunting has lost its appeal. Instead, I set out game cameras and find excitement viewing the captured images. A spring-fed trout pond sits off the end of my runway, but I watch the fish feed and spawn instead of fishing.

Beth and I feel so fortunate that we ended up in Maine, and would never leave. We also have derived great pleasure from our alternative lifestyle. And, best of all, memories are forever!

ACKNOWLEDGMENTS

As Beth and I neared retirement, we accepted a part-time job as caretakers of a island camp. Soon, we were good friends with the owners, Juliet Kingsmill and Charlie Hogan, who lived most of the year near London, England. Juliet was intrigued by our Hardscrabble stories. She gently encouraged me to write a memoir, something I never had considered. After sharing the first tale, Juliet urged me to continue. Over the next several months her enthusiasm was infectious. Thanks, Juliet.

Tracy Hart (Editing with Hart) deserves a big thank you. My first attempt to write these tales yielded a dry account of facts. Tracy taught me how to breathe life into the stories. She was a great coach! Every time I reread a section her many hints jump off the page. Thanks Tracy.